THE VERMONT EXPERIENCE

THE VERMONT EXPERIENCE

In Words and Photographs

TEXT SELECTED & EDITED BY
SUSAN BARTLETT WEBER

INTRODUCTION BY TOM SLAYTON

PHOTOGRAPHS BY
VERMONT LIFE CONTRIBUTORS

Vermont Life
Montpelier, Vermont

Photograph Page 2:

Cultivation — both of the land and of the spirit — has helped define Vermont since its earliest days.

Strafford.

Jon Gilbert Fox

Printed in the United States of America. First edition.
1 2 3 4 5 6 7 8 9 10

Book design by The Laughing Bear Associates, Montpelier, Vermont

Library of Congress Cataloging-in-Publication Data

The Vermont Experience/Selected & edited by Susan Bartlett Weber: introduction by Tom Slayton; photographs by Vermont Life contributors.
   p. cm.
   Bibliography: p.
   ISBN 0-936896-08-6 : $29.95
   1. American literature — Vermont. 2. Vermont — Literary collections. 3. Vermont — Social life and customs. I. Weber, Susan Bartlett. II. Vermont life.
   PS548.V4V47 1987
   810'.8'032743 — dc19
                                 87-21640
                                   CIP

CONTENTS

Introduction, 7

Spring, 14

Summer, 44

Autumn, 84

Winter, 112

Spring, 140

About the Authors, 147

Acknowledgments, 151

Books for Further Reading, 153

I think we are the last true regionalists, or
maybe — who knows? — the first of a new breed.
Not local colorists, at any rate, not keepers of
quaintness for quaintness sake. We're realists.
And realism means place, and place means where
we are.

Hayden Carruth
Brothers, I Loved You All,
1978

INTRODUCTION

 "The gods of the hills," declared Vermont hero Ethan Allen more than two hundred years ago, "are not the gods of the valley." I know what he meant every time I return home from a trip, drive up the White River Valley or the Champlain Valley, see the Green Mountains rise around me, and feel the quiet welcome they give.

Even today, two centuries after Allen's famous remark, Vermont remains a place apart. There is something unusual, even unique here, bounded by water and mountains and given a French name that doesn't quite translate. ("Vermont" — the literal translation means something like "mountain of worms." To be "Green Mountains," which is obviously what was intended, it would have to be "Verdmonts.") Gertrude Stein is reputed to have once said of Oakland, California, "There's no *there* there," meaning that it was as characterless as a place could be. Vermont, we can at least agree, has plenty of "there."

Everyone has his own view of why Vermont is whatever it is. This book offers a sampling of two centuries of comment about the life actually lived in the Green Mountains, and the ideals that life has inspired. In assembling it, we chose voices from literature, historical writings, diaries, travelers' journals, poetry and prose alike, and illustrated our selections with contemporary photographs, many of which have appeared in *Vermont Life* Magazine over the past ten years.

As we brought texts and photographs together, we came to feel that though Vermont has changed and is changing still, there are constants. Out of the complex fabric that we call the Vermont experience, a few simple threads have lasted, to be woven into our daily lives. This is true despite the tremendous changes that have come to Vermont in the past fifty years — despite air travel and interstate highways, ski resorts, suburbs, computers, network television, social changes and all the rest of it.

Consider just a few of many contemporary expressions of the past that live on today: Vermont is no longer primarily a farming state, yet the farming heritage still shapes both the landscape and our attitudes. American society has grown distinctly non-Puritan. And yet the Vermont character remains shaped by its Puritan heritage: the real religion of most Vermonters is work, and the pursuit of pure pleasure is still looked upon with distrust, even scorn, by those not doing the pursuing. Although most people now protect themselves from nature to an almost embarrassing degree and can change the temperature in a room with the turn of a thermostat, the land and weather retain much of their importance to those of us who live here. We value the beauty of our pastoral landscape for its own sake and have enacted a strong body of environmental law to safeguard that beauty and the ecological integrity of which it is the visual expression. Winter is still a challenge to most of us and remains a great social leveler as well; Alexandr Solzhenitsyn, the internationally known author who lives in Cavendish, chops

firewood for heat, just as most of us do. Literally thousands of Vermonters can work a team of draft horses — and in Franklin County alone, where the tradition has remained particularly vital, there are several hundred working teams.

Many, many other examples exist, as anyone knows who has ever done backyard maple sugaring or gone to a rural auction. Much more than simple cultural artifacts, these continuing traditions are living expressions of the past, linking present-day Vermonters with those who preceded them on this land.

It would be pleasant to pretend that the values of Vermont are eternal, but they are not. The modern world has eroded them considerably, and in many instances we are the poorer for the erosion. But though its heritage is undeniably threatened, Vermont is fortunate in having a living heritage and values it can call its own. Many places in the United States are much the poorer for losing touch with theirs.

Consider but a single art form that links Vermont to its past, its wealth of fine architecture. Like any other art, architecture is an expression of ideas, and Vermont's old buildings are exceptionally rich in ideas. Not only do they express their various eras, they speak of the philosophies, goals, esthetics, sublimities, and pomposities of those eras. There are Vermont barns that copy the style of nineteenth century factories and factories that copy Italian villas; Congregational churches that mimic Greek temples and village residences designed to look like Gothic forest retreats. And there are buildings like the Strafford Town House that in their own way speak volumes.

The Town House, as eloquent a building as any in the state, stands with consummate poise and authority at the north end of the Strafford village common. It has been there in its chaste

clapboard siding and pure-white paint since 1779, when it was erected, the first building in the village of Strafford. Not a little of its undeniable authority — it is the dominant structure on the green and stands watch over the buildings nearby as if they had been gathered to it by sheer force of character — is due to its siting, atop a small hill. It expresses a transcendent dignity that somehow manages to avoid being overbearing, because it is both graceful and restrained.

Below the bell tower, the old structure is almost completely devoid of ornamentation, except for the pilasters on its large central doorway. The building proper is all lines and angles, a dissenter's meetinghouse in style, plain and austere as Puritan doctrine — except for its remarkable Federal belfry, which is constructed entirely of thin columns, arches, and delicate, wedding-cake railings. Somehow it all coheres, the fanciful belfry uniting in balance and harmony with the foursquare reticence of the frame structure it tops. The building stands at the head of Strafford's common like the pure ideal of a church — a world — reformed.

"Why in these early times, with all the problems of sustenance and survival and striving with the soil and the forest and the elements, did they resolve to make all that effort to raise these massive timbers to get a 24-foot ceiling?" asked Rochester architect William Huntington in a 1972 report on the building for the Strafford Historical Society. "Why put up a 100-foot tower with top stages so light and open, so daring against the power of winter storms? Would it not have been much more practical to build a small, low, warm place to meet in? Why build a cathedral?"

His answer was that the human spirit's search for beauty is illogical — and inspired. The Town House still presents, he wrote, "an uplifting message of life and truth."

It is common today to think of institutional religion as merely confining. But the religion of Vermont's colonial settlers was inseparable from their lives. Far from oppressing them, their religion provided much of the shape and meaning of their existence. The town's first church (there were rather quickly others) dominated the green both physically and symbolically by design; it was the physical manifestation of the village's faith, opposing with order and light the dark and menacing wilderness that surrounded it.

And there can be no doubt that Strafford was faced with a wilderness. It was actually later, in 1789, that the Rev. Nathan Perkins, a cultured Hartford, Connecticut, minister, traveled to Vermont and wrote grimly about getting lost in the wild forests:

"Got lost twice in ye woods already — heard ye horrible howling of ye wolves," Perkins wrote. "Far absent in ye wilderness — among all strangers — all alone — among log huts — people nasty, poor, low-lived, indelicate — and miserable cooks."

Yet a decade before the fastidious reverend wrote, the Strafford Town House had been built upon its little hill, facing down the glowering woods around with a beauty that must have been as welcome to frontier Strafford as doctrine to the faithful.

Two centuries later, we have a different feeling about wilderness, because it is now as scarce in both America and Vermont as architectural elegance was in 1779. We value it and set tracts of it aside to keep wild forever. Yet there is an inevitability about nature. The forests, radically cleared for 150 years, have lately returned to the vicinity of the Town House, and as I look at the old building, again surrounded by trees, I think of two continuing aspects of the Vermont experience.

The untamed forest was and is the emblem of the dark and fertile natural world, vigorous, unrefined, perhaps a bit frightening, even today, yet ever-perfect in itself; "the force that through the green fuse drives the flower." That force

Strafford Town House.

Jon Gilbert Fox

expresses itself in a human attitude as well as in nature. Call it Vermont Druidism; it is personified as Green Mountain Mary in Genevieve Taggard's wonderful poem, "The Nursery Rhyme and the Summer Visitor" (page 57). No crop need be taken from Green Mountain Mary's overgrown field; her "use" of the field is simply to delight in the unrestrained life that the resurgent forest symbolizes. Today, there is no shortage of contemporary Green Mountain Druids. The worship of nature for its own sake is a constant in Vermont, because nature itself has always been so omnipresent here.

This view contrasts with the way of seeing and ordering existence that the Strafford Town House represents: an idea of civilization turned by virtuoso carpentry from wood and stone into shining white structure. The ideals of the Enlightenment and the strictures of religion can be seen in its frame and spire; it expresses order, balance, and restraint, the hand-built superego of a society of high ideals pointing heavenward, seeking a new and better world.

Like Strafford's wooden cathedral, all of New England has been shaped by its Puritan past and a heritage of conscience, high ideals, and (their natural counterpart) guilt. As Elizabeth, my Northeast Kingdom-born wife, is fond of saying, "Guilt makes good citizens." Her joke has more than a touch of truth. Though Vermont was rugged, rough-and-tumble, and open for the taking, Puritan beliefs and ideals flourished here, and firm idealism is still a recognizable part of the Vermont personality. It has had to be. Determination and the ability to work toward distant goals were surely needed to clear the first rough fields from the primordial Green Mountain forest. They are needed even today, to forge one's way through the depths of a Vermont winter.

Ideals help people survive difficulty. And ideals have consequences; it is no accident that Vermont's contribution of soldiers to the Civil War was higher on a per capita basis than any other state's save one. George Perkins Marsh's

10

edict that the earth was given for usufruct, not waste (page 33), is linked directly to the Puritan view of the earth as divinely ordained for humanity's use. Calvin Coolidge's meditation on the death of his son as the price exacted for the attainment of the presidency (page 79) likewise springs from a Puritan source. And the high moral thought of Robert Frost or Dorothy Canfield Fisher expresses our slightly compulsive idealism perfectly.

It may seem that Green Mountain Mary and Calvin Coolidge see fundamentally different aspects of Vermont: the wild and the tamed. Yet with the perspective of history, we now know that these two views balance one another and are interwoven of necessity. The forest is not antithetical to the Strafford Town House, after all. The understanding of that truth is one of the gifts of modern ecological science, which owes much to the early work of Marsh and his farm-boy's upbringing in Woodstock. In the works most characteristic of Vermont, its writers, artists, and historians have expressed a similar balance. Humanity is seen not as all-dominant but as a part of nature; we must cooperate and work with the world but treat it well, if we are to survive.

The poems of contemporary poet James Hayford express that tempered view. The squashes he grows in his garden are surprising in their pure beauty, yet "worthy to win prizes" — ready, that is, to meet the ever-present standards of a watching, measuring world. And he raises the question of choosing one point of view or the other when he asks in "Processional with Wheelbarrow" (page 39):

"What are we out to celebrate —
The Force that makes seeds germinate,
Or the Grace that makes man meditate?"

He ultimately awards the day to nature, as most Vermont writers do, especially the modern ones. Fortunately for all of us, the tension between the given world of nature and the world of humanity's creation has lasted long enough to produce both the beauty of the

Strafford Town House and the wisdom of James Hayford's poetry.

Such themes of balance and counterpoised extremes can be found throughout the Vermont experience. That may be so because of the influence of pastoralism, our most persistent myth — and our most fitting one.

Pastoralism is a good dream, an ideal that has fascinated humanity down through the ages, appearing in civilizations from ancient China to classical Greece, to Renaissance England, to contemporary America. It is the dream of a farmed Eden, called by the Greeks Arcadia. Significantly, pastoralism is founded on a profound duality; it implies both civilization and nature. The country exists as a respite from the city. Wild nature is present, but held at bay by cleared and cultivated land. The emblem of pastoralism is the tamed, unspoiled middle landscape of fields and hedgerows. Its symbol is the farm. And although Vermont did not invent the idea of a simple rural life where humankind can rediscover its natural goodness, the idea has flourished here, as the art and literature of the Green Mountains amply illustrate. It has brought many new Vermonters to this state and kept many natives, even though both are well aware that the dream and the reality are often out of synch with one another.

There are still links between the real Vermont and the beloved ideal. That is one of the reasons it remains such an interesting place. True enough, farming for a living is not a romantic tumble down the nostalgic halls of yesterday. It is a practical business proposition, currently cut close enough to the bone to drive many farmers to despair — especially when they see the farm down the road sold to newcomers who consider farming a pleasant weekend pastime. And yet, the most practical dairyman must occasionally see the land as something more than a good investment, well managed. A love of land and

12

"Vermont does have a lot of old-time values," says folklorist Eleanor Ott of Calais. "But there's also a lot of folklore and nostalgia about those values nowadays, too."

The folklore is interesting and important, Ott believes; but it is also important to her that we recognize the threat that careless nostalgia and sentimentality pose to the genuine virtues of this genuine place. "If we don't recognize the threat, we're in danger of losing the values," she says.

In other words, Vermont has been discovered and is now accessible. It must live in the present, and preserve its singularity here and now.

How can that be accomplished? No one should presume to give a precise answer to that question, any more than anyone can successfully define Vermont itself. But if, as I believe, it is our values and traditions that make us what we are, and if those values and traditions spring ultimately from the land and the people who live upon it, then we must keep both land and human heritage alive to preserve in some recognizable form the Vermont we know and love.

The fortunate thing is that the rediscovery of Vermont is usually a delightful, eye-opening experience, as I think this book amply shows. This state has, in addition to its abundant natural beauty, a living culture, history, and folk traditions that are appealing and beautiful. Its attitudes are resilient, and spiced with wisdom and humor. Like the landscape, its human heritage demands care and conservation, but offers a rich repayment for our efforts. The Vermont experience deserves to be preserved, and more than preserved, lived.

Tom Slayton
Vermont Life Magazine

animals, crops and the daily drama of weather are part of the pastoral myth to be sure; but they are also part of the unusual human equation that makes for a good farmer. And well-farmed land, lately becoming a scarcer commodity here, is the essence of the pastoral landscape we all love. So there are connections, even today.

But the modern world and mass culture now pose a distinct threat to Vermont's uniqueness, simply because there is so much of the modern world-at-large and so little of Vermont. The state's mountain-locked isolation, which kept it out of the cultural mainstream for many years and gave it time to develop its own traditions and atmosphere, has ended. Vermont is within a day's drive of more than twenty million people, and the resulting pressures have revamped the economy, threatened the integrity of the Vermont countryside, and changed the lives of all Vermonters profoundly. What may be less obvious is that Vermont's values are also under pressure and in some cases are being compromised.

SPRING

JOURNEY FOR THE NORTH

When we arrived at our place of
residence where we intended to make
a settlement, I had only one axe
and an old hoe with which to begin clearing land
and growing crops. That first summer I cleared
about two acres with only an axe, my one
remaining ox being too sick to be of any help
at that time.

Mountains and hill farms, valleys and bottomland
and in the bottom, always, water,
rivers and streams,
white and rocky, slow and muddy,
and in the bottom also, always, villages, because —
grist mill, saw mill, creamery —
power, log course, sewer.

Now, half of what they were a hundred years ago,
but still inhabited
by the beast who sleeps at night and walks upright,
in a landscape overwhelmed still
by something other than
what we have made,
by mountains and valleys,
water and sky, open land
and trees.

David Budbill
Down to the Village, 1981

TOWN MEETING

In a mountain town with flash-floods roaring over the banks of its water-courses after hard rains, bridges have an imperious priority. Our bridges needed reinforcement, not only from recurring high water, but against the great tonnage of modern traffic.... It would take all the resources of a poor mountain town to keep our bridges in repair. To add to that expense the enormous cost of a new school — insane!

...The little flickering flame of responsibility for the future of the town's children died down to a faint glimmer in the hearts of the men and women whose votes would in a few moments make the decision. Those who had longed and worked for the school sat silent, disconcerted by the predicted crashing of the bridges, loud in their ears. What could be said against that?

Then up sprang Patrick Thompson.... He had worked his way up to partnership in one of our two grocery stores. What education he had — it was sound — he had received in our public schools. We usually saw him in a white apron, standing behind the counter, selling sugar and tea.... We still remember his exact words... "We are being told that our town cannot afford to keep its bridges safe and also to provide for its children a preparation for life that will give them a fair chance alongside other American children."

"That's what we are being *told*. Not one of us here really believes it. We just can't think what to say back. But suppose it were true — Then I say, if we have to choose, 'Let the bridges fall down!' What kind of a town would we rather have, fifty years from now, a place where nitwit folks go back and forth over good bridges? Or a town with brainy, well-educated people capable of holding their own in the modern way of life? You know which of those two is really wanted by every one of us here. I say, '*Let the bridges fall down!*'"

...It was a turning point in the life of our town. We spoke not a word. We sat silent, thinking. And feeling. What we felt, with awe, as though we saw it with our physical eyes was in all our human hearts, the brave burning up to new brightness of the ideal.

Presently the Moderator said in the traditional phrase, "Any further discussion?"... Then "Forward your ballots." In a silent line the grave-faced voters moved slowly toward the ballot box, each hand holding a white paper.

The school was built.

Dorothy Canfield Fisher
Vermont Tradition, 1953

THE FIRST GOOD RUN

Sugaring usually begins in mid-March and runs until mid-April. These dates are anything but fixed, however, the weather being what it is. This past spring the first good run in Thetford didn't come until almost the end of March (we were having sub-zero mornings almost up to St. Patrick's Day), and most of us closed down around April twenty-fourth. A few diehards kept boiling until the first of May.

One joy of sugaring is that you take advantage of the inconstant weather. In fact, the more capricious the weather — the more spring seems to come and then dances away again — the better the sugaring. You can't do it at all without freezing nights and warm days, which is why the attempt to set up a maple industry in England in the eighteenth century failed: an English spring is too gentle. But it goes further than that. A late wet April snow is simply frustrating for the motorist, or a suburbanite impatient to get to work on his lawn. For a syrup maker it is a cause for rejoicing, because maples run their fastest on such a day. Most of the season you do well to get three or four inches of sap in the bottom of each bucket over a twenty-four-hour period, but on the day of a sugar snow your best buckets fill to the brim and run over. That night you boil until midnight, and there is a holiday atmosphere.

Noel Perrin
Third Person Rural,
1983

Late sugar snow lies wet upon a maple grove in Peacham as a man and his team collect sap from metal buckets.

Richard W. Brown

21

24

MAPLE SWEET: THE SUGARMAKER'S SONG

Sugaring is doubly sweet because it means the end of winter. It is special because it marks the rare and hopeful time between winter and spring. And it is expensive because of all the toil, care, and coopera- tion it demands and the fact that it takes about forty gallons of sap to make one gallon of syrup.

When you see the vapor pillar
Link the forest and the sky
Then you'll know the sugarmaking
Season's drawing nigh.
Frosty night and thawy day
Make the maples' pulses play
Till congested by their sweetness
They delight to bleed away.

Chorus:
Then bubble, bubble, bubble, bubble, bubble goes the pan.
Furnish better music for the season, if you can.
See the golden billows, watch their ebb and flow;
Sweetest joys indeed we sugarmakers know.

And for home or love or any kind
Of sickness it's the thing.
Take in allopathic doses
And repeat it every spring,
Till everyone you meet
At home or on the street,
They'll have half a mind to bite you
For you look so very sweet.

Upper:

Sheldon.

Paul O. Boisvert

Left:

Richard W. Brown

Middle:

Near Orwell.

Janet Mullins

Lower Right:

Shelburne.

Paul O. Boisvert

As sung by

Margaret MacArthur

An Almanac of New England Farm Songs, 1982

THE STINGIEST MAN

I cannot speak for the other two Duffus children, my older brother and my younger sister; but I myself could not be called devout and I don't recall that the others were, either. We liked church suppers, whether they provided baked beans, oyster stews, or maple sugar on snow with pickles and doughnuts; we liked anything good to eat; we also liked sociability within certain limits.

For this reason I think we, all of us, at one time or another, went to the Wednesday evening prayer meeting with my mother. Once we even had a religious cat, which followed my mother to church and up the stairs to the Sunday School room, where the prayer meeting was held, and sat on her lap, purring loudly, throughout the service. This must have been during the Reverend Blake's time, because Reverend Jasper Pell, the old war horse who followed Mr. Blake, would have regarded the presence of a cat as sacrilegious.

But Mr. Blake, as I am sure it was, stopped and petted the cat as he came down the aisle after saying the benediction. "That's a good Congregational mouser," he said....

This was a pleasant incident, but things were always happening at prayer meeting. Once in a while somebody would start to, as we said, get religion; but neither Mr. Blake nor Mr. Pell, unalike though they otherwise were, cared much for emotionalism. We were expected to take our religion soberly, and not to shout about it in public.

The best way to stop anybody from getting religion too loudly at a prayer meeting in the Congregational Church in Williamstown was to call for a hymn. If Mr. Ainsworth was present, and he usually was, there was noise enough then.

Still, a prayer meeting was different from the regular Sunday morning service. It was more informal. In theory, anyhow, anybody present could offer a prayer or a personal statement, which he couldn't do, of course, Sunday mornings. The minister became a sort of moderator. I found this interesting, the way a play was, or an adventure book, because you never knew what would happen next.

So I would remember, even if there were not other reasons, the night Deacon Slater got up and said he had been doing a lot of praying lately. He was, he said, a naturally stingy man, maybe the stingiest man in town. He had been praying to the Lord to help him overcome this weakness, and he thought he was making some progress.

There was quite a silence when Deacon Slater sat down, because the truth seemed to most persons about as he had stated it. He really was a stingy man, perhaps the stingiest man in town.

Mr. Blake promptly called for a hymn.

I asked my mother on the way home what Deacon Slater meant and if he really was as stingy as he said.

She debated with herself for a while. Finally she shook her head. "If he was," she concluded, "he wouldn't say so."

Robert L. Duffus

*Williamstown Branch,
1958*

Children who live in small Vermont towns have the chance to see firsthand the cycle of the year in nature and in the evolving lives of their neighbors and friends.

Norwich.

R.J. Alzner

27

MUD SEASON

That year the mud was so deep that my poor old father had to use snowshoes on the road. As he approached the village he seen a hat lying on that muddy road which, as he came nearer, he observed to be moving. In some consternation, he picked up the hat to find the head of his friend and neighbor, Walter Wheeler.

"Walter," said my father, "you're in trouble, ain't you?"

"No," said Walter, "for I still have my horse under me."

Francis Colburn

Letters Home and Further Indiscretions, 1978

Before spring can really come there must be mud season, those few weeks when the thawing back roads turn into mucky obstacle courses and every ditch becomes a stream. The brief interlude tests everyone's resolve, even as it holds out the promise of the true spring ahead.

Opposite Page:

Richard W. Brown

Upper Right:

Janet Steward

28

SONGS AND SNAKESKINS

Spring makes nearly every creature exuberant, it seems. A friend, canoeing in Vermont, noticed a granddaddy snapping turtle, as big as a washtub, swimming alongside his craft for possibly a mile, with a curiosity the turtle no doubt is going to lose after a few more canoeists go by. A bear emerges to graze the tender meadow grass in his back field as early as 5:00 P.M., and the cow moose that likes to eat pond weeds in the marsh downhill from him can hardly be scared away before eight in the morning — these being the daylight feeding hours that moose and bear preferred before they had so many human neighbors to contend with.

Spring is the time when beasts stoke up after the hardships of the winter, and when birds court a mate and stake a territory. Some of the most beautiful birdsongs are contentious in intent. The flicker's speedy, bouncing flight as it crosses a clearing to pound its bill on a dead limb, the woodcock's yo-yo courtship display, spiraling high and plummeting — these are part of the inimitable panache of spring. Yet how can one explain the search great crested flycatchers make for a snakeskin to weave into the lining of their nests? Where snakeskins have become hard to find, they substitute a scrap of cellophane. The bird is only robin-sized, but surely a seasonal and talismanic exuberance is involved here.

Our friend must scratch his blackfly bites, which also go with spring, and sometimes will wake up at 3:00 A.M. to a dead, wintry chill. He loads wood into the stove and reassures himself that he is on the younger side of middle age and, furthermore, that this is May. With dawn, the vireos and song sparrows strike up and say indeed it's so.

Edward Hoagland

The Tugman's Passage,
1981

30

THE GIVEN EARTH

Man has too long forgotten that the earth was given to him for usufruct alone, not for consumption, still less for profligate waste.

George Perkins Marsh
Of Man and Nature, 1864

For all Vermont's hilly contours, much of its soil is fertile, well-drained and profitable to farm, even today. The farming heritage remains intact, and continues to remind visitors and natives alike of the good things that country life has to offer.

Reading.

Constanti Kazak

A Place for Strange Gods

I can't remember exactly what I saw the first time I went to a bog, but I do recall my wonder at the strangeness of it all. Suddenly I had entered a new world. Perhaps my sensations were primed by what I had read about bogs, but most came as original revelations. And most of what impressed me *was* sensation: the spongy undulations of the mat, the subsidence of each of my steps, the subtle yet arresting colors of rain-glazed sphagnum mosses, the gnarled forms of seemingly ageless plants. Nor was my imagination cheated: The day was noiseless and draped with storm clouds; a fog will-o'-the-wisped up and over a leaden pond; the place seemed to throb with deep energy, buried under a gray mantle of solitude. Some strange gods had to be living there.

That first encounter plucked some sonorous chord within me, and subsequent trips to other bogs, whatever their size or the season, never dulled the magic of that first song. From then on bogs were my unearthly music, and I listened. In the years since, I have studied bogs both scientifically and casually, trying to understand the maker of the music. In this search for understanding I have been like anyone else who cherishes a piece of the world as his own, wanting still to experience the special feelings yet seeking to know more.

No matter how much we know or think we know about bogs, we cannot fully appreciate them if we only read the score and never listen to the music. Mountains, oceans, forests, and bogs are more than places to those who love them. They have hearts like hibernating animals, beating imperceptibly yet vitally.... Bogs keep diaries from their births, recorded page upon page in their peats. Their histories remain secrets for hundreds or thousands of years, until we literally dig deeply to reveal them.... It is a natural history of the "personalities" and relationships produced by the plants and animals that helps make bogs living systems.

The fact that men have walked on the moon does not mean that poets can no longer write about it; it is still a sacred part of the heavens. So with bogs on earth. While the scientist in us seeks to understand them, the poet in us wants to keep them away from complete discovery, safe in some shadow of mystery.

Charles W. Johnson
Bogs of the Northeast, 1985

35

SPRING

Down Route 2, the farmers
are hauling hen-dressing
in flat, open wagons.
The stink is terrific.

The fields on either side
fan out in long arcs
of mud and shiny stubble;
even the crows, laboring
from tree to tree,
seem fresh, and everything
is ready to start over.

So a tractor heaves off
over the shallow bank,
and the farmer hums
or whistles, thinking
of his cows, his taxes,
or his woman, while today
paints a first wash of red
over his face and forearms.

Saddled to his big John Deere,
he throws the spreader switch,
flinging the stuff
in every direction, then rides on
through the stench and roar
like a free man, like a man
on top of something other
than a half-ton
of chicken shit: like how
you imagine a rich man, maybe,
with his money.

Linda McCarriston
Talking Soft Dutch, 1984

36

38

PROCESSIONAL WITH WHEELBARROW

With every move I've made today
Four lambs paired up to lead the way,
Or follow, in high-tailed array.

To an unheard overture
We're marching with manure
In rites that seem obscure.

What are we out to celebrate —
The Force that makes seeds germinate,
Or the Grace that makes men meditate?

From the arch look on the features
Of four of us five creatures,
I'd say the day was Nature's.

James Hayford
The Furniture of Earth,
1976

*Sheep, one of the founda-
tions of Vermont agriculture
in the nineteenth century,
faded from the farm scene,
but today they are back, in
a more modest way, raised
for both wool and meat.*

Windsor.

Ava Emerson

VERMONT'S VIRTUES

I like Vermont because it is quiet, because you have a population that is solid and not driven mad by the American mania — that mania which considers a town of four thousand twice as good as a town of two thousand, or a city of one hundred thousand, fifty times as good as a town of two thousand. Following that reasoning, one would get the charming paradox that Chicago would be ten times better than the entire state of Vermont, *but* I have been in Chicago, and have not found it so.

Sinclair Lewis
1929

The leaves of spring usher a young cyclist down the streets of Glover, population 850. Vermont's small towns and villages make it, statistically, the most rural of all states; about two-thirds of its residents live in towns of less than 2,500.

Paul O. Boisvert

MARSHALL WASHER

... I see a man with a low-bent back
driving a tractor in stinging rain, or just as he
enters a doorway in his sheepskin and enormous
mittens, stomping snow from his boots, raising
his fogged glasses. I see a man in bib overalls
and rubber boots kneeling in cowshit to smear
ointment on a sore teat, a man with a hayfork,
a dungfork, an axe, a 20-pound maul
for driving posts, a canthook, a grease gun.
I see a man notching a cedar post
with a double-bladed axe, rolling the post
under his foot in the grass: quick strokes and there
is a ringed groove one inch across, as clean
as if cut with the router blade down at the mill.
I see a man who drags a dead calf or watches
a barn roaring with fire and thirteen heifers
inside. I see his helpless eyes. He has stood
helpless often, of course: when his wife died
from congenital heart disease a few months before
open-heart surgery came to Vermont, when his sons
departed, caring little for the farm because
he had educated them — he who left school
in 1931 to work by his father's side
on an impoverished farm in an impoverished time.
I see a man who studied by lamplight, the journals
and bulletins, new methods, struggling to buy
equipment, forty years to make his farm
a good one; alone now, his farm the last
on Clay Hill, where I myself remember ten.
He says "I didn't mind it" for "I didn't notice it"
"dreened" for "drained," "climb" (pronounced *climm)*
for "climbed," "stanchel" for "stanchion,"
and many other unfamiliar locutions; but I
have looked them up, they are in the dictionary,
standard speech of lost times. He is rooted

in history as in the land, the only man I know
who lives in the house where he was born. I see
a man alone walking his fields and woods,
knowing every useful thing about them, moving
in a texture of memory that sustains his lifetime
and his father's lifetime. I see a man
falling asleep at night with thoughts and dreams
I could not infer — and would not if I could —
in his chair in front of his television.

Hayden Carruth

Brothers, I Loved You All,
1978

SUMMER

BISMARCK ON VERMONT

In the year 1878 three American gentlemen were visiting Prince Bismarck at his residence of Friedrichsruhe. In the course of the conversation Bismarck said to them: "I would like to give you my idea of a republic. I think you will grant that I am somewhat of a student of political history. My idea of a republic is a little State in the north of your great country — the smallest of the New England States — Vermont." One of the Americans said, "Not Massachusetts?" "Ah, no," he answered, "Vermont is small in area, of slow growth, has a larger percentage of school attendance than any other State, is not devoted to manufactures nor so much to farming as to make its interests political, owes nothing to the general government for Civil War expenses, and aims primarily and purely at the educational and religious evolution of each individual. Is it not true," he added, "that this little State keeps its senators and representatives in office term after term until they die?" and he proceeded to speak of Collamer and Morrill and Edmunds. One of the Americans rose and said: "Your Excellency, two of us are graduates of the University of Vermont and one of us claims that State as his birthplace." Bismarck himself rose and said: "Gentlemen, you should be most proud of your inheritance. To be a son of Vermont is glory enough for the greatest citizen."

Robert D. Benedict

Burlington, 1905

47

WHY GROW WILDFLOWERS?

In the farthest corner of my father's pasture was a small wood lot of sugar maples, birches, hop hornbeam and pignut hickory, growing on rocky, ledgy ground. The cows were usually turned out to pasture the last of April and it was my work and that of old Shep to get them down to the bars in time for milking every night. Usually their bovine obstinacy would prompt them to linger in this small wood lot in the far end of the pasture to make Shep and me as much work as possible in getting them. But in this little grove of hardwoods there were quantities of Springbeauties, Hepaticas, Bloodroot, Violets, Squirrelcorn and Dutchmans-breeches, which so entranced the young man of eight years that it was occasionally necessary for some older member of the family to not only come after the cows, but Shep and me as well.

One night I dug and brought home a clump of Dutchmans-breeches and planted it under the lilac bush. I know now that blossoming time is not the proper time to move Dutchmans-breeches, but Providence looks after those who know no better, and that clump lived in its new home for nearly twenty years before the suckers of the lilac finally obliterated it. This was the first wild gardening I ever did.

It has been a good many years since I have been after the cows and listened to the silent but impressive sermons preached by Jack-in-the-pulpit or stained my face and hands with the juice of the wild strawberries, but the friendly feeling for the wild things of the woods and field which I acquired in those philosophical younger days has persisted. I always regarded the wildflowers of the woods as members of the family and rather felt it my duty to look after them as far as possible, while they in turn would impart many secrets which could never be learned inside the schoolhouse walls.

Great changes have taken place in our New England hills since I moved that clump of Dutchmans-breeches. Groves of great trees, under whose branches the dainty people of the woods lived and thrived, have been cut for lumber, and in their place a maze of young growth so thick that only here and there are the wildflowers, formerly so abundant, able to survive. The open pastures are being covered with sapling growth of birches and pine not yet old enough to furnish shade and shelter for our woodland flowers, but just large enough to choke out the flowers of the open fields…

And then our roads. They are better, much better than we used to have, but this very fact has had disastrous results for many of our wildflower neighbors. Even from distant cities the automobile brings friends and relatives to the farmer's home on Sunday afternoon and when they leave the back of the car may be laden with, besides tired human beings, masses of Laurel, Azaleas, Columbine or Arbutus, and our roadsides become so much poorer. I would not for an instant deny the people the right to enjoy and love our wildflowers, but the sad part of the story is that the loveliest wildflowers are being almost exterminated in the most accessible places.

48

What are we going to do about it? Well, some of us have spent a great many years thinking over this problem. Passing laws does not do any good because with the permission of the land-owner anyone may gather wildflowers under the protection of the Constitution. Posting land on the part of estate owners may preserve these plants, but where they may be enjoyed by comparatively few people.

I believe that all human people need close association with nature's people, so it seems to me that the only satisfactory answer to this problem is to tell folks how to grow them.

George D. Aiken

*Pioneering with
Wildflowers*, 1968

THE TELEPHONE

"When I was just as far as I could walk
From here today,
There was an hour
All still
When leaning with my head against a flower
I heard you talk.
Don't say I didn't, for I heard you say —
You spoke from that flower on the window sill —
Do you remember what it was you said?"

"First tell me what it was you thought you heard."

"Having found the flower and driven a bee away,
I leaned my head,
And holding by the stalk,
I listened and I thought I caught the word —
What was it? Did you call me by my name?
Or did you say —
Someone said 'Come' — I heard it as I bowed."

"I may have thought as much, but not aloud."

"Well, so I came."

Robert Frost

The Poetry of
Robert Frost, 1968

STEEP HILLS AND WILD STRAWBERRIES

The old homestead was to the south of the common, it was a long, two-story white frame house with narrow windows and a green front door, upon which there was a curious brass knocker, and a brass door-plate bearing the name "Gen. Martin Field." Above this front door was an archaic window or transom in the shape of a fan. Three acres of ground were around the house — a large front yard and a side yard and an orchard (for my grandfather was an amateur naturalist), a wood-shed, a barn, an ice-house and a carriage-house. In the carriage-house was a monster chaise, and I used to wonder whether there ever was a horse big enough and strong enough to haul it. There was a long gravel walk leading from the front gate to the front door, and on each side of this walk there was a flower-bed, in which, at the proper season, prim daffodils bloomed. On the picket fence which divided the front and side yards there was a sun-dial, and just to the north of this dial stood a sassafras tree — you see I recall these details, although twenty-five years have elapsed since I last visited the old homestead in Vermont. How true and good it is that the scenes of childhood never fade from our memories.

There were hills all around the little village, and there were trout brooks that crept furtively through woods and thickets; and, my, how steep those hills were, and how sweet the wild strawberries, and how cool and pungent the checkerberries were that nestled away up there in that gravelly, sterile soil! On the east side of the mountain flowed the West River, a black and turbulent stream, in ill repute with all solicitous mothers, for Reuben Fisher's boy Lute was drowned therein in the summer of 1823, and Lute's grave in the burying-ground on the hill near the Stedman farm was studiously and solemnly pointed out to every little boy who evinced a disposition to hook off and go swimming. By common consent the only proper place for little boys to go swimming was in the brook just this side of Burdette's melodeon factory on the Dummerston road. The village was called Fayetteville then: now it is Newfane.

Eugene Field
The Woman Who Most Influenced Me: My Grandmother, 1890

52

MRS. APPLEYARD'S APPLE-TREE CHEESE

Vermont possesses an ideal climate for growing apples. The soft white blossoms, like these in Randolph, are a lovely bonus.

Marjorie Ryerson

Perhaps another tree would do, but an apple tree with its stout curved twigs sticking out so handily, its low-hung branches, its dapple of sun and shade, is the Cream Cheese Tree, *par excellence.*

This cheese is made of cream that has thickened well and is only slightly sour. To make it Mrs. Appleyard brings new milk, fresh, frothing, ivory-colored, slowly to a temperature of 150 degrees F., keeps it there for half an hour, and then pours it into a scalded milk pan. She likes to have at least four quarts. She sets the pan in a warm place for twenty-four hours. By then the cream should have risen so that most of it can be easily skimmed off without getting much milk. She then puts four thicknesses of cheesecloth over a bowl and pours the cream, which she has beaten a little with a fork, on the cheesecloth. Now she ties the cloth together at the top with a strong piece of string. Being a string-saver she has no difficulty in finding an appropriate piece. There is some that belonged to Hugh's kite that has been helpful for many years. It was Mr. Appleyard's string first.

The cream should be thick enough so that not much will drip through the cheesecloth, but she carries the bowl along through the winter kitchen, the summer kitchen, and the woodshed. Then out into the warm July afternoon and to the Dutchess apple tree, which is reaching out a curved twig just right for a cheese-hanger. If she has chosen the right day — and usually with the same instinct that makes goldfinches wait for thistledown to build their nests, she has — the cheese will be ready by the afternoon of the next day.

There will have been no blazing heat by day, no thunderstorms, no dank chill at night, but under the apple tree a warm green-and-gold twilight all day, a breeze just strong enough to rustle the leaves and dry the gently swinging bag, only the thinnest clouds across the stars at night. If there is a moon it shines with warmth and softness. At dawn there is silver mist down the valley, and when the sun comes out there will be cobwebs on the grass.

Louise Andrews Kent
Mrs. Appleyard's Kitchen, 1942

54

THE NURSERY RHYME AND THE SUMMER VISITOR

Green Mountain Mary, Green Mountain Mary
What does your garden grow?

Violets, moss, ground pine, goldenrod, briars,
Strawberries, spirea, wintergreen, ferns,
And a little bit of grass, alas.

Will you sell me your meadow?
        Oh, no.

Who crops it?
        Deer.

See, here, Green Mountain Mary, you people are very, —
Excuse me —
Queer.

Genevieve Taggard
A Part of Vermont, 1945

Fletcher.

Bob Davis

MAKING DO

We seldom bought anything out of season, such as asparagus, strawberries or corn. Instead, we enjoyed thoroughly each food as it came from the garden. We began early in the spring with parsnips, the first thing available in our garden. As soon as the snow went, we dug them and had them for one meal a day for about three or four weeks. During that period they provided much of our starch and sugar. With parsnips went salsify, celery and parsley root, leeks and chicory. Then came six to eight weeks of asparagus, accompanied by dandelion, chives and multiplier onions. Before the asparagus was finished we had begun on spinach, radishes, mustard greens, garden cress and early lettuce. Following that we had green peas, beets, standard lettuce, string beans and squash. In the height of the season came corn, tomatoes, shellbeans, broccoli, cauliflower and celery. As autumn approached, we turned to the cabbages, winter squash, turnips, rutabagas, carrots, escarole, Chinese cabbage, collards, with cos lettuce, fall radishes, spinach and beets, and for the first time, potatoes and dried beans. We cultivated strawberries, raspberries and blueberries and ate them in season. These berries also grew wild in abundance, along with chokecherries, shad and blackberries. For other fruit we had pears, plums and apples.

After the snows, when the gardens were white and frozen, we turned to our vegetable cellars with their winter roots, cabbages, winter squash, potatoes, beets, carrots, turnips, onions, rutabagas, celery root, parsley root and pears and apples. The hardiest of these vegetables would still be fresh and edible up to the time the snow melted and we were digging parsnips once again.

Helen and Scott Nearing
Living the Good Life, 1954

PLOWING, HARROWING AND PLANTING

The haying that has just been completed on this farm near Woodstock is one of any successful farmer's many summer tasks. More than any other group of people, Vermont's farmers help keep the landscape open and beautiful. Although they are uncompensated for this service, except through the profits of their farms, it benefits everyone who enjoys Vermont's characteristic interplay of field and forest.

Russell Schleipman

After turning out time came the ordinary spring work: plowing, harrowing and planting. That was very particular work with Gramp, because his greatest pride was his garden and his crops, specially his corn. His corn come first, and then his garden had to look just so, with the rows perfectly straight and the potatoes hoed exactly right.

When he put me to dropping potatoes, instead of dropping them I had to plant them. He gave me a stick so that I could measure from one hill to the next. If I asked how big he wanted the hill, he always said, "Make it big enough to hold a half-bushel of potatoes." You have no idea what a lot of dirt that takes. Not that he ever expected to get so many potatoes, but he just liked to be sure.

You think of the ordinary farmer as kind of careless about the look of things, but Gramp wasn't like that. As I say, all the rows had to be as straight as a string, and he made me take a ruler to the potatoes even though he wouldn't eat them after they was grown; and besides that, he always raised a few cucumbers just because they grew pretty, and he liked to see them grow. He wouldn't eat them either, because he said the hogs wouldn't touch them, and he wouldn't eat anything a hog wouldn't eat. All he got out of them was the satisfaction, and if anybody came along that wanted any, they could have some.

All his crops must be hoed by hand before the fifteenth of June because that was the start of haying. Unless the haying is done before the first of August, it's practically no use; it's no good after that. The hay is too ripe, just gone to seed, mostly fiber, and hardly worth cutting. There's no real food value to it by then.

Walter Needham
A Book of Country Things, 1965

Rupert

H.S. Johnson

GRAVITY FEED

In summer when the afternoon begins to turn
slowly letting go of each color,
the dog and I go out for one last outing in the field.
She runs off on some rich scent —
loses it and circles back, then loops away
through the tall grass
like a hand sewing.

When I reach the top of the hill
the sun hangs directly above our house.
It notches the roofline, then drops
making one window
flash on the inside like a signal.

Coming back at dark I can see my daughter
dancing alone in her room to the radio.
I roam around the yard, studying the lines
of the house, trying to absorb its shape.
I wait until the very last to be drawn
into the bright spill of the windows.

Tom Absher
Forms of Praise,
1981

65

ON LAKE CHAMPLAIN

Lake Champlain, a 110-mile-long slice of water eleven miles wide at widest, was the arena for French and English rivalries during the early history of North America. Ethan Allen's last homestead is one of many historic sites near its shores.

South Hero.

Richard Howard

And so we go cruising down the lake and past an island or two I'd like to buy. In place of Indians, the summer boy and girl camp canoes dart here and there, miles from land, though a thunderstorm hovers.

And it isn't the history or the people past or present. It's the lake itself. In storms the waves dash in on the grey old boulders and wash the points of long red rock and gurgle and spout in the cliff caverns. What we like is sand beaches and miles of stone; the hidden harbors and cliffs of deep black depths beside bent-strata rocks that arch and twist into red somersaults; the miles of blue, with a sun that makes you squint, and a fair breeze that bends the mast; the hayfields by the water, and the cows and apple trees; daylight sinking orange behind the Adirondacks; or dawn coming pink from behind Green Mountain peaks; the tent in a cove where wavelets tinkle all night; stars, cool swims, hot noons; white squalls and glassy calms; always the beauty and danger. All you can do is feel it tingling down your arms and into your mouth and eyes and nostrils like drops of crystal and radish and salt.

Elliott Merrick

Green Mountain Farm,
1948

WHERE COMFORT IS KING

For the summer camper-out there is no camping ground more desirable from every point of view than the Vermont shores and the islands of Lake Champlain. In this region, which is indeed a paradise for those who love to fish and hunt and camp, are many delightful camping spots and a score of established summer camps. One may rent a camp complete or rear his own canvas home and live happily until snow flies where "style is dead and comfort's king." With boating, bathing, fishing — there are plenty of perch, pike, pickerel and black bass in Champlain — driving or automobiling over the hard beach roads, one can pass a most delightful vacation here. This section is exempt from mosquitoes and other insect pests, and what is still more remarkable there are no fogs and one may sit on the lake shore in the early morning or evening with as much safety and comfort as at noon. All of the most attractive summer camps of Lake Champlain are reached from Boston and New York by the Central Vermont Railway Line.

Central Vermont Railway
brochure, 1917

A Visit to Burlington

It was a bright forenoon, when I set foot on the beach at Burlington, and took leave of the two boatmen, in whose little skiff I had voyaged since daylight from Peru. Not that we had come that morning from South America, but only from the New York shore of Lake Champlain. The highlands of the coast behind us stretched north and south, in a double range of bold, blue peaks, gazing over each other's shoulders at the Green Mountains of Vermont. The latter are far the loftiest, and, from the opposite side of the lake, had displayed a more striking outline. We were now almost at their feet, and could see only a sandy beach, sweeping beneath a woody bank, around the semi-circular bay of Burlington. The painted light-house, on a small green island, the wharves and warehouses, with sloops and schooners moored alongside, or at anchor, or spreading their canvas to the wind, and boats rowing from point to point, reminded me of some fishing town on the sea-coast.

While we stood at the wharf, the bell of a steamboat gave two preliminary peals, and she dashed away for Plattsburgh, leaving a trail of smoky breath behind, and breaking the glassy surface of the lake before her. Our next movement brought us into a handsome and busy square, the sides of which were filled up with white houses, brick stores, a church, a court-house, and a bank. Some of these edifices had roofs of tin, in the fashion of Montreal, and glittered in the sun with cheerful splendor,

Church Street, Burlington.
Paul O. Boisvert

imparting a lively effect to the whole square. One brick building, designated in large letters as the custom-house, reminded us that this inland village is a port of entry, largely concerned in foreign trade, and holding daily intercourse with the British empire. In this border country, the Canadian bank-notes circulate as freely as our own, and British and American coin are jumbled in the same pocket, the effigies of the king of England being made to kiss those of the goddess of liberty. Perhaps there was an emblem in the involuntary contact. There was a pleasant mixture of people in the square of Burlington, such as cannot be seen elsewhere, at one view: merchants from Montreal, British officers from the frontier garrisons, French Canadians, wandering Irish, Scotchmen of a better class, gentlemen of the south on a pleasure-tour, country squires on business; and a great throng of Green Mountain boys, with their horse-wagons and ox-teams, true Yankees in aspect, and looking more superlatively so, by contrast with such a variety of foreigners.

Nathaniel Hawthorne
New England Magazine, 1835

A City's Spirit

When Ira Allen first saw the curving shoreline and pine-covered hills south of the point where the Winooski River flows into Lake Champlain, he saw potential for a city. Today, Burlington, a center for commerce, education and the arts, fulfills his vision.

Carolyn Bates

We claim for Burlington the prevalence of a social equality, as complete and untrammeled as can be found in the smallest country village anywhere in New England. Intelligence, virtue, and a reasonable degree of good manners, will at once admit a newcomer of any rank or occupation into any circle which he or she may choose to enter.... In the dwellings, the household economy, the gardens and grounds of our wealthy families, you will see much good taste and considerable luxury of a substantial kind, but there is no prevalent fondness for display in dress, or equipages, or fashionable entertainments. As compared with many villages its size, Burlington is rather a staid, old-fashioned place, in its social characteristics. If a man wishes to be held in high honor for his money, or a wife for her elegant attire, let them by no means come to Burlington.

Abby Maria Hemenway

The Vermont Historical Gazetteer,
1868

August

The afternoon air is so still and heavy with heat
everyone in the house has gone off to nap.
I let the tap water run a while over my finger tips
waiting for the cold stuff to come from the spring.
Bulkhead clouds appear in the kitchen window, comically grand.
Time settles over the edges of the house like a glass dish
and except for the white butterflies flashing in the tall grass,
the world seems to have stopped.
This could be the very moment
when the shrubs and weeds will have reached their full growth.
As the water cools in my hand a silence works its way
down through the hayfield, across the yard and into the house.
It is in my presence. I can feel it with the tiny bones in my ear.

Tom Absher
Forms of Praise, 1981

*Corn ripens on Lake
Champlain's Grand Isle.
The Champlain Valley and
the lake's islands hold
some of Vermont's best
farmland.*

Richard Howard

QUIET

I like to sit down with a book in a quiet room, sure of uninterrupted time in which to savor its wisdom, beauty, gaiety, sadness....

Dorothy Canfield Fisher
The Lady from Vermont, 1971

Shrewsbury.

Jon Gilbert Fox

IF I HAD NOT BEEN PRESIDENT

Sunderland.

Paul Miller

My own participation was delayed by the death of my son Calvin, which occurred on the seventh of July. He was a boy of much promise, proficient in his studies, with a scholarly mind, who had just turned sixteen.

He had a remarkable insight into things.

The day I became President he had just started to work in a tobacco field. When one of his fellow laborers said to him, "If my father was President I would not work in a tobacco field," Calvin replied, "If my father were your father, you would."

After he was gone someone sent us a letter he had written about the same time to a young man who had congratulated him on being the first boy in the land. To this he had replied that he had done nothing and so did not merit the title, which should go to "some boy who had distinguished himself through his own actions."

We do not know what might have happened to him under other circumstances, but if I had not been President he would not have raised a blister on his toe, which resulted in blood poisoning, playing lawn tennis in the South Grounds.

In his suffering he was asking me to make him well. I could not.

When he went the power and the glory of the Presidency went with him.

The ways of Providence are often beyond our understanding. It seemed to me that the world had need of the work that it was probable he could do.

I do not know why such a price was exacted for occupying the White House.

The Autobiography of
Calvin Coolidge, 1929

79

RUINS UNDER THE STARS

All day under acrobat
Swallows I have sat, beside ruins
Of a plank house sunk up to its windows
In burdock and raspberry cane,
The roof dropped, the foundation broken in,
Nothing left perfect but axe-marks on the beams.

A paper in a cupboard talks about "Mugwumps,"
In a V-letter a farmboy in the Marines has "tasted battle..."
The apples are pure acid on the tangle of boughs,
The pasture has gone to popple and bush.
Here on this perch of ruins
I listen for the crunch of the porcupines.

Galway Kinnell

Flower Herding on
Mt. Monadnock, 1964

Economic change has left
some Vermont farmhouses,
like this one in Waterville,
abandoned and sinking
into their foundations.

Kindra Clineff

HARVESTING THE SQUASH

Among the great surprises
is harvesting the squash:
When I pull up my vines
I marvel at what rises
Out of dense leaves, weeds, grass:
Squashes unseen till now,
All different shapes and sizes,
All worthy to win prizes.

James Hayford
At Large on the Land,
1983

*Although much of Vermont
is stony and unproductive,
the state boasts regions of
great fertility in the Champlain Valley, the valleys of
the Lamoille, Missisquoi
and Connecticut rivers,
and in the eastern Piedmont
section.*

Right:

Hanson Carroll

Opposite Page:

Carolyn Bates

AUTUMN

THE VILLAGE

There it lies
dozing peacefully under the maples;
A church, a school, a tavern, some stores,
And a matter of fifty houses…
A sleepy village in a peaceful valley,
Yet, friend, there life stages its drama…
Fifty houses offering the life of the race.

Walter Hard

*A Matter of Fifty
Houses,* 1952

Whiting.

Clyde H. Smith

Photograph Pages 84-85:

The horse pull is a tradition at county fairs throughout New England. A well-matched team can move a prodigious amount of weight and produce considerable drama into the bargain. Contenders and the curious watch the action at the Enosburg Dairy Festival.

Paul O. Boisvert

Falling Off

In the afternoon the air smelled of earth and apples. I looked at my woodpile and I thought — as I think every October first-frost — that it looked too small.

I went to the woodlot and cut dry limbwood for my cookstove and made a deal with a neighbor to cut another cord for me in exchange for several cords for him. From the garden I rescued the last of my onions and cucumbers. I dug a bushel of potatoes and brought in three wheelbarrowsful of pine twigs for kindling, and one wheelbarrowful of pumpkins that had been growing wild all summer on the old manure heap below the barn. There seemed to be a thousand things which needed doing, all at once, though I thought I had been harvesting and bringing things in for weeks.

Diane Kappel-Smith

Wintering, 1984

Left:
Ryegate.

Richard W. Brown

Upper Right:

Frank S. Balthis

Lower Right:

Richard W. Brown

THE VIEW FROM THE HILL

I put up sandwiches and a quart of beer, and toward noon we started out through the meadow behind the house. The sun was well up and hot but the meadow was still wet from the dew, and when we crossed through the high grass at the lower end she held her dress high so it wouldn't soak through and the sun glistened on her legs above her knees where the wet grass brushed against them.

At the very top of the hill, under the scattered beech trees that Lucien had left standing, we turned around and looked back. We could see down through the meadow to the back of the house and barn, on past the building to the lower pasture, where the cows were grazing, small and still in the grass, below the pasture to the bright yellow sugar maples and beyond them to the county road winding out of the trees down to the lake. We could see the whole length of the lake, five miles, and the mountains sheering up out of the water on both sides, and in places the county road cutting thin and curving along the east side. The mountains were red with soft maple and yellow and white with birches a thousand feet up their sides, then blue-green with firs rooted tight into cliffs where you would say trees couldn't grow. For maybe a whole minute Alabama looked at the lake and the mountains.

Even after I had sat down in the grass under a beech tree she kept looking. Finally she spoke. "I reckon," she said, "that is so much more than any picture machine that I about have to believe it."

She sat down beside me without taking her eyes off the view, as though it might disappear if she looked away for even a second, like something you are watching go across the sky at night or like a buck that you cannot quite get a good line on through the woods. Then she said, "I reckon that is why you stay up here, all right. Because anytime you want you can just step out the door and see all these colors."

Howard Frank Mosher

Where the Rivers Flow North,
1978

Spectacular fall foliage is the result of gradual changes over weeks, not of a sudden cold snap. In Vermont, the reds and oranges of sugar maples predominate. Their effect is heightened by the yellows in the birches, the red of the swamp maple, and the unchanging evergreens. Here, the season reaches its climax in Tunbridge.

Jeremy Dickson

90

A VISITOR'S OPINION

The whole country of Vermont will in process of time be extremely difficulted to fence their land. There is no good fencing timber as in Connecticut. Stonewall can never be made. The mountains are rocky, but too steep to carry the stone into the valleys.

Nathan Perkins

*A Narrative of a Tour
Through the State of Vermont,
April 27 to June 12, 1789*

*An old wall, built stone
upon stone by Cavendish's
first farmers, follows the
maples that line the road.*

Chuck Place

THE COVERED BRIDGE HOUSE

Grafton.

Gail Elyse DuBoise

Because there's a race
For living space,
I have a wonderful scheme.
I'm planning to own a covered bridge
Up over a running stream.
Except for some doors on entry halls,
I'll board up the ends with planks
And put some windows upon the walls
That face away from the banks.

No buildings are apt to crowd me there
With nothing to build them on;
And, since my yard will be waves and air,
I won't need to mow the lawn.
I'll have a skylight where raindrops skid
And clouds look in as they sail
And cut a floor hole (one with a lid)
For filling my water pail.

And though, in winter, I'll skate a lot
Or read from morning till twilight
Before I climb on my cozy cot
To watch the moon through my skylight…
In spring, I'll open my floor hole wide
And fish through it for my supper
And later scrape the scraps in the tide,
Or — if I'm a cleaner-upper —

I'll hang my pans in a net on string
And maybe my laundry, too;
And when it's summer, I'll swim and sing
or paddle my red canoe.
And if the shivering mice sneak in
When summer changes to fall,
I'll say to each mouse:
"Enjoy my house.
There's room enough for us all."

Kaye Starbird
*The Covered Bridge
House and Other
Poems,* 1979

THE LAST WORD OF A BLUEBIRD AS TOLD TO A CHILD

As I went out a Crow
In a low voice said, "Oh,
I was looking for you.
How do you do?
I just came to tell you
To tell Lesley (will you?)
That her little Bluebird
Wanted me to bring word
That the north wind last night
That made the stars bright
And made ice on the trough
Almost made him cough
His tail feathers off.
He just had to fly!
But he sent her Good-by,
And said to be good,
And wear her red hood,
And look for skunk tracks
In the snow with an ax —
And do everything!
And perhaps in the spring
He would come back and sing."

Robert Frost

*The Poetry of
Robert Frost*, 1968

A GOLDEN MOMENT

And just for the record, the foliage peaked this year precisely at 3:38 P.M. on Thursday, September 29. I was there when it happened. I was fishing by the elementary school, and had stopped to stare in awe at the trees. There were dark storm clouds overhead, the wind would be stripping most of the leaves off by dusk, but for now the black sky framed perfectly the bittersweet reds and yellows, giving them a color so vibrant and urgent that their radiation was a tug on the heart.

As I watched, something remarkable happened. The sun found a hole in the cloud just large enough for the one crepuscular ray to leap through. It slanted obliquely toward earth, catching a gold tree on the bank and casting its radiance onto the surface of the river, spinning it gold. My fly rode on its shimmer for the space of a yard — for that one fleeting moment I was fishing a golden fly for golden trout on a golden river. Then the cloud clamped shut around the sun, and the peak was passed.

I heard voices up on the bank. A boy and girl, each about eight, were kicking through the leaves piled against the trees. Every few yards they stooped to pick one up and put it in a plastic bag they jointly carried.

They waved, and came over to watch me. As it turned out, the leaves were for their oldest sister, in college out west. She was homesick for Vermont's autumn, she had written; they were collecting a bagful of the yellowest yellows and the reddest reds to send her to cheer her up.

"Here's one for you," the girl said, handing me a maple leaf.

"Thanks, I'll keep it on my desk this winter. It will remind me of September."

The boy saw his chance.

"September," he said, spreading his arms apart as if to embrace the smells, the colors and light, "is my best favorite year."

W. D. Wetherell
Vermont River, 1984

The lakes and ponds of Vermont range from tiny to grand, from specks of blue tucked away along mountain ridges to one of the nation's largest, Lake Champlain. This fall excursion, punctuated by a view of a swamp maple at its autumn peak, took place on Eligo Pond in Craftsbury.

Richard Howard

VERMONT IS A STATE I LOVE

Vermont is a state I love. I could not look upon the peaks of Ascutney, Killington, Mansfield and Equinox without being moved in a way that no other scene could move me. It was here that I first saw the light of day; here I received my bride; here my dead lie pillowed on the loving breast of our everlasting hills.

I love Vermont because of her hills and valleys, her scenery and invigorating climate, but most of all, because of her indomitable people. They are a race of pioneers who have almost beggared themselves to serve others. If the spirit of liberty should vanish in other parts of the union, and support of our institutions should languish, it could all be replenished from the generous store held by the people of this brave little state of Vermont.

Calvin Coolidge

Bennington, 1928

Plymouth.

Fred M. Dole

99

TIME TO PLANT TREES

Time to plant trees is when you're young
So you will have them to walk among —

So, aging, you can walk in shade
That you and time together made.

James Hayford

At Large on the Land,
1983

Marshfield.

Kenneth A. Wilson

DRIFTS OF LEAVES

The autumn wind roars through the maple tops, ripping the foliage to shreds, shouldering the trees. It is big and careless and bluff and hurts a little already, and doesn't care. It makes me think, not just of the coming long winter, but of the old philosophies of joy and pain, while the tree limbs writhe and roar and the leaves fly down by the thousands. Walking the little old dirt roads at this time of year, you come round a bend and wonder where the road lies, it is so deep under drifts of red and yellow leaves.

Elliott Merrick

Green Mountain Farm, 1948

Paul O. Boisvert

A Parable

And that reminds me of the parable of the golden retriever. It seems Walter Wheeler bought himself a retriever — one of them duck-retrieving dogs — and he went out the first morning of his proud ownership and went duck hunting. He went into his duck blind. A herd of them ducks went over. Walter lifted his gun and he shot one of them ducks and the duck went into the water and that dog retrieved the duck, but how did he do it?... that dog walked along the top of the waters and retrieved that duck. Walter was somewhat taken aback, but he said to himself. "I *was* in Hardwick last night. And I stayed kinda late. I stayed till almost ten o'clock. I better not decide about this thing until tomorrow."

So he waited until the next morning and he went out again shooting ducks and he shot a duck and the dog indeed retrieved the duck by walking along the top of the waters. By this time Walter was kinda scared, and he called his neighbor Foster Kinney up and said, "Foster, I got an awful odd acting dog. I'd like you should come duck hunting with me tomorrow morning and see if I'm wrong about this dog." And Foster said, "I will as soon as my chores are done," and he did. And the next morning they both went into that duck blind and they both shot a duck and that dog walked along the top of the waters and retrieved both of them ducks. And Walter looked at Foster and said, "I told you they was something wrong with that dog. Will you tell me what it is?" And Foster looked at Walter and said, "There's nothing wrong with your dog. It just can't swim."

Francis Colburn
Letters Home and Further Indiscretions, 1978

THE GREEN MOUNTAIN PARKWAY

Mt. Mansfield's snow-dusted upper slopes tower over Pleasant Valley farms as fall takes a turn toward winter. Rugged as they may appear today, Mansfield and the rest of the Green Mountains are believed to be remnants of a range that was once as high as the Himalayas.

Clyde H. Smith

In Favor

The question of whether or not the State of Vermont should co-operate with the Federal government to the extent of providing the right-of-way for a National Parkway to extend along the Green Mountain Range for the entire length of the state will be settled by the freeman voters of the state in town meetings on the first Tuesday in March. I believe this is one of the most important questions that the voters of Vermont have been called upon to decide in many years. The decision that will be made at that time, I believe, will be far-reaching in its effect upon the future prosperity of the state and its people.

I fully realize that this is a controversial question, that there are many people whose views are directly opposite from those that I entertain and that they may be right and I may be wrong, but I am nevertheless convinced that the construction of this proposed Green Mountain Parkway by the Federal government along the Green Mountain Range is one of those really great opportunities that is rarely presented to a state and its people.

…How long are we going to continue to see Vermont money used to help develop and build prosperity in other states and refuse to take advantage of an opportunity to participate in it ourselves? How long are we going to listen to that siren song about keeping Vermont unspoiled?

Ernest H. Bancroft
The Vermonter, 1936

Opposed

The proponents of the Parkway want to carry Vermont into an intense commercialization of its mountain scenery and summer attractions. The opponents represent a school of thought which prefers to have the state's development follow along more traditional lines…

It is along traditional lines that I believe the State should move for many reasons. In a day when there is confusion, clamor, and uproar all around us, we should cling to our traditional peace; in a day when wise men from New York and Burlington are telling us how to be saved, we should stick to our old faith that men are saved by calm consideration of what actually is and not what others promise us shall be; in a day when fever is in the air, we should keep our temperatures down; in a day when men are inclined to follow loud voices promising and prophesying golden things, we should listen to the cautious, careful leaders whose voices are not loud, and keep in mind the warning of the western cattleman that when a herd is stampeding, the real leaders are never in front — they are back in the herd because they cannot see what all the racket is about: and, as a last hint, we might as well remember what our fathers learned among these Vermont hills long ago — that there are no new roads to Paradise — not even a Parkway.

Arthur Wallace Peach
The Vermonter, 1936

MY NOVEMBER GUEST

Fayston.

Ann Day Heinzerling

My Sorrow, when she's here with me,
Thinks these dark days of autumn rain
Are beautiful as days can be;
She loves the bare, the withered tree;
She walks the sodden pasture lane.

Her pleasure will not let me stay.
She talks and I am fain to list;
She's glad the birds are gone away,
She's glad her simple worsted gray
Is silver now with clinging mist.

The desolate, deserted trees,
The faded earth, the heavy sky,
The beauties she so truly sees,
She thinks I have no eyes for these
And vexes me for reason why.

Not yesterday I came to know
The love of bare November days
Before the coming of the snow,
But it were vain to tell her so,
And they are better for her praise.

Robert Frost
*The Poetry of
Robert Frost,* 1968

A Certain Comfort

The trees in the woods stand in an anticipatory hush. After the green rush of spring and summer productivity, after the celebratory brilliance of the fall, comes an interim of relinquishment and fatigue. In the time that follows the trees take on a quality of stripped-down mutual readiness, almost an eagerness, for the oblivion of winter. Is it fanciful to think that they know what is coming? They seem so wise in their silence, standing in expectant ranks as far as the eye can see uphill and down dale, so true to themselves and loyal to one another, possessed of a knowledge so much more ancient than any known to us, so accepting of their duties and all weathers and seasons. Standing amongst them, that restive newcomer, the human being fraught with questions and distractions, finds in their calm assurance a certain comfort in the November dusk.

Lee Pennock Huntington

Hill Song, 1985

A WINTER SKY

A country road lit by the
setting sun curves across
fields in Jeffersonville.
Looming above is Mt. Mansfield, an arctic outpost
where winter arrives first
and lasts longest.

Peter Miller

Behind our back the golden woods
Held the gold of a great season
As we lay on the shore of the woods
And watched the long afternoon
Dying in golden light in the woods.

Before us the brown marsh
Brought the dark water, dry grass,
Cattails, waste of the close-cropped marsh,
And the hunters' blinds were watching
For traffic on the blinded marsh.

It had been a long, beautiful fall
And as we sat on the shore remembering
The season behind us, the golden fall,
One of us said to the other
There may never be an end to fall.

Then two ducks flew away from winter
And a gun reached out and caught one
And dropped it like snow in winter,
And without looking back or understanding
The first flew on alone into winter.

We rose as dusky light filled the woods
And looked out over the brown marsh
Where a dog swam and where the fall
Covered the land like a winter
And winter took fall from the marsh and woods.

Galway Kinnell

*The Avenue Bearing
the Initial of Christ
in the New World,
1953*

111

WINTER

A Winter Diary

Mon. Nov. 14, 1887

Temp. 5 A.M. 27°   *8 P.M. 33°*

A warm thawey day the snow went a little 186th Day of work for Mr. J.S. Brown. Besides a helping to do the milking I and Henry T. Brown went up on the Hill, the white Lot next to C.C. Halls place a Choping and drawing together with the Oxen Trees down and once in to then piled we guess their is 4 cords of 4 foot wood when cut up Mr. Brown and Charles killed 2 Hogs for J.S.B. today Looks like a storm tonight I am in hopse their will be a rain but not a flood

Tues. Nov. 15, 1887

Temp. 5 A.M. 32°   *Noon 40°*   *6 P.M. 33°*

A snowey day soft and dauby some 3 inches more 187th Day of work for Mr. James S. Brown Esq. In the fore noon I helped to weigh off the 2 Hogs also got a load of straw & put in the Hogpens. Then Chas. W. Blanchard & I Cleaned out the lower Barn floor of corn stalks 2 loads put them in the upper Barn also ground my axe and several knives This after noon He & I went to Parkers & Pipers Steam Mill above the Union and got each of us a load of Saw dust with Oxen and Steers Chores as uasual Mr. J.S.B. went to Ludlow today with 23 Hogs dressed weight 430 and 392 2 Tubs of Butter. Old Doctor Morgan was burried today aged 49 years His son Field is a Doctor Harrison Sumners wife taken Laudreum to Kill Her Self today

Wed. Nov. 16, 1887

Temp. 6 A.M. 34°   *Noon 36°*   *8 P.M. 29°*

Cloudy and windy thawey 188th Day of work for Mr. J. S. Brown I cut one Maple Tree beside the fence across the meadow East side of cornfield drawed it home with Oxen 2 loads of on the long Sled Worked up part of it into stove wood helped to milk Mr. B. and Charles have been working on the Shead also making feed racks Henry a choping on the white lot Hill Allen J Brown He is here to his Father's tonight

The Diary of Hyde Leslie
Plymouth Notch, 1887

Opposite Page:

Snow. It is the cover hiding winter's imperfections, and its pleasures are limitless. However, it must also be shoveled.

Left:

Richard W. Brown

Right:

Timothy J.E. Keeler

East Corinth.

Hanson Carroll

OLD MAN PIKE

Michael Bouman

Old man Pike was a sawyer at the mill
over in Craftsbury.
He lived just down the road from here.
Every morning he walked six miles through the woods
over Dunn Hill saddle while the sun rose.
He took dinner and supper in the village
then walked home across the mountain in the dark.
Sally Tatro who used to live on my place
would hear him coming through the night, singing.
Sometimes he'd stop to gossip
but mostly she only saw him stride by the window
and disappear.

The old man could have stayed home,
milked cows, like everybody else,
but he needed an excuse to go and come
through the mountains, every day,
all his life, alone.

Old man Pike didn't believe in the local religion of work,
but out of deference, to his neighbors maybe,
he bowed to it,
placed its dullness at the center of his life,
but he was always sure, because of his excuse,
to wrap it at the edges of his days
in the dark and solitary amblings of his pleasure.

David Budbill
The Chain Saw Dance,
1976

DRIED APPLE PIES

I like good bread; I like good meat,
Or anything that's fit to eat,
But of all poor grub beneath the skies,
The poorest is dried apple pies.

Chorus:
I loath, abhor, detest, despise,
Abominate dried apple pies.

The farmer takes his gnarliest fruit,
The wormy, the bitter, and hard to boot.
They leave the hulls, to make you cough,
And don't take half the peeling off.

(Chorus)
Then on a dirty cord they're strung,
And from some chamber window hung,
And there they serve a roost for flies
Until they're ready to make pies.

(Chorus)
Tread on my corns and tell me lies
But don't feed me dried apple pies.

As sung by
Margaret MacArthur
*An Almanac of New England
Farm Songs*, 1982

MOUNTAIN PHILOSOPHY

The White Mountains glow above a lone house in Caledonia County, its apple-tree swing and wash lines waiting for spring. A visitor to Mt. Mansfield, right, savors the special pleasure of late winter sun by the mountain's chairlift.

My parents dreamed a mountain, and bought it, and made it into the resort where I learned to ski. Pico stands apart, one of the tallest peaks in the Green Mountains; a realm radiant with discovery and my parents' exuberance; the first ski resort in North America to have an Alpine lift. I was too young to know that I was growing up with the development of American skiing; mother and father kept our worlds apart. And yet in time and reflection Pico grows. It looks the way a child would draw a mountain, a rounded triangle with symmetrical sides and a smooth top. Each winter Pico seemed to rise; deciduous trees bared its contours, white, translucent under snow and long angled light. Emanations of Pico's glimmering heights caught me up in the triangular exchange between God, man, and nature. Very early I began to understand that mountains are never there simply to ski and climb. They shape the long line of my approach as past and prologue. They shape the way I see them as metaphors of physical mastery and spiritual possibility.

Andrea Mead Lawrence
A Practice of Mountains, 1980

Opposite Page:

Richard W. Brown

Right:

Sandy Macys

A Cool Morning in Vermont

It's a rare Vermont winter that doesn't have one stretch of weather when it's twenty below every night, and not much above zero even at midday. Keeping warm during such a spell is either difficult or expensive — sometimes both. If you're living in a big old house in the country, and if you have an oil furnace, you've got roughly three choices. You can keep the thermostat up at 70 and go broke. You can turn it down to 55, put your family in long underwear, and shiver. Or you can heat two or three rooms with wood stoves, and move in, relying on the furnace only to keep the rest of the house from freezing. That's what most of us do.

Last winter, though, my old farmhouse was getting a long-promised remodeling. The little wood stove that normally sits in the corner of the kitchen and the big one that normally dominates the living room were both out in the barn, surrounded by dismantled stovepipe. My wife and daughters had gone on a trip for the three weeks we'd be without a kitchen. I was alone in the house, doing the fifty-five-and-shiver routine.

One specially cold morning I woke up with an uneasy feeling. The house was deathly silent. No distant cellar hum of the furnace, no comforting purr in the hot-air ducts. Pausing only to put on my long underwear (and a wool shirt, and wool pants, and a sweater, and heavy socks and boots), I ran downstairs. We have a thermometer in the living room. Thirty-seven in there. We have another on the front porch. Twenty-six below zero out there. I figured I had maybe two hours before the house began to freeze.

I hurried down cellar and began pushing every start and restart button I could find on the furnace. Silence as before. I circled the furnace again, found a small red button on the left side, and jammed it hard. The blower sprang to life. I ran upstairs. A chill wind was pouring through the ducts. Not a trace of heat. And ten minutes gone already.

Back down to poke at the furnace some more. Then I suddenly remembered the oil tank. I made it across the cellar in two jumps, and looked at the gauge. Empty.

While I was on the phone to the oil company, the church clock in the village (half a mile away) struck eight. As it struck, Heman Durkee and his son Heman, Jr., the two carpenters who were remodeling the kitchen, arrived. They were just in time to hear my cry of anguish when I learned that the delivery truck had already left on its morning rounds. The manager would try to catch it at its next stop, but even if he did, it would be 30 miles away. He couldn't promise what time it would get to me, except to assure me that it would be in the forenoon.

A Cool Morning in Vermont

Heman is tempermentally a stoic. "Guess we can work just as well in our coats," was all he said to me as he and his son stood watching their breath form in the kitchen. But Heman, Jr., frankly prefers creature comforts. "Didn't you have a little stove in here?" he asked.

Ten minutes later we had the stove set up on the sub-flooring, the pipe run up, and a good fire of carpenter scraps going. Then the three of us staggered in with the big old parlor stove, and set that up. It's a great gothic-looking stove made in Rutland about 100 years ago, and it will take two-foot logs up to about nine inches in diameter. Before I had to leave for work at quarter to nine, the living room was practically warm, and a few wisps of heat were even floating upstairs toward the two bathrooms and all their tender pipes.

Heman called me at work around eleven to say that the house was safe. The oil truck had come and put 258 gallons into my 250 gallon tank. Though he is not only stoic but taciturn, he added something else. "Guess you're going to save a little money," he said.

"How is that?"

"Don't they give you the first 50 gallons free, when they let you run out?"

I hadn't known that. But it's true. They do. Whether they would have insisted if I hadn't brought the matter up, thanks to Heman, is another question.

In fact, I saved more than that. Heman, and Heman, Jr., kept the little kitchen stove going every day, until the actual morning came to put the new floor down. By then, the cold spell was over, and we were having a thaw.

They never said it was as a favor to me. Or to keep them warm. Perhaps it wasn't. "That much less scrap to take to the dump," Heman explained.

Noel Perrin
First Person Rural,
1978

126

Snowy Afternoon

Sometimes in winter there comes a spell of snowstorms and sunshine and terrific contentment. On snowy afternoons there is a special blessedness in saying, oh it is too snowy to chop wood this afternoon. And the gray snow sifts down, and one takes off one's boots and sits by the fire and is glad of the way the wool socks smell; and a pie is baking in the oven, and the gray snow is sifting down.

Or one gets tired of that and goes out into the silent woods where the snow is whispering down through the bare branches, and plugs through the drifts, up the hills, past the cliffy ledge that is almost always clear of snow, in among the thick firs, across the brooks that are filled so deep you wouldn't know they are there. Here is the place where I had a fire yesterday. One stands on the cold hill in the icy wind looking off across the dimness at the shadowy mountains lost in the snowstorm, and one thinks. What does one think of? Oh, nothing much, just thoughts. And then it's good, going home to the fire and the creeping night, and Kim home from school on his skis, his cheeks very red, and he very hungry, and the darkness comes, and one is glad everybody is home over the twelve-foot drifts. It is simple and it is enough.

A snowy wind rips through Westford.

Bob Marinace

Elliott Merrick

Green Mountain Farm,
1948

WINDHAM THAW

Magellan braved the seas that roll,
Commander Perry found the Pole,
Leander swam the Hellespont,
But *I* have tramped across Vermont
And known far more about rough weather
Than those three worthies put together;
And the bitterest weather that ever I saw
Was what they called, "a Windham thaw;"
And if you'd learn what that might be,
     Listen to me:
The wind comes down from the north-northeast
At sixty miles an hour at least,
Bringing a sweep of snow and hail,
Freezing the milk in the foaming pail;
Great boughs crack in the hemlock grove;
Men sit close to the red-hot stove;
The storm cloud sinks, the storm cloud lifts,
Horses wallow among the drifts,
The carter stamps to save his toes,
Icicles hang from the postman's nose;
Every blast has a tooth and claw,
The farm boy's cheek is red and raw,
Never a rooster dares to craw,
Towser cowers beneath the straw,
The snow whirls up in a williwaw,
For the devil is beating his mother-in-law,
And that's what they call "a Windham thaw!"

Arthur Guiterman
Green Mountain Verse, 1943

LOVE OF SNOW

In those years, days like this
When storm made the oak leaves hiss
Were days of winter bliss:

Pulling our sleds to the top
Of town where houses stop
And fields and pastures drop

Over back to farms and the river,
We'd slide and climb forever —
Till first dark made us shiver;

Then homeward tired and slow,
Ready for kitchen glow,
All white from love of snow.

James Hayford
At Large on the Land,
1983

Norwich.

Nancy Wasserman

Opposite Page:

North Hartland.

John Sherman

KITCHEN JUNKETS

It took a while to do the barn chores in the winter, so it was apt to be about nine o'clock before one could get to the dance... back in those days one had to figure on traveling from five to ten miles going and coming home. Many times the roads were drifted with snow and a sharp wind would be blowing over Sheffield Heights. The roads were rolled instead of plowed, and often the track was marked through the fields with tall sticks....

If it was a bad storm, my dad would be quite stubborn about letting me go out into it, and would recite the tragic poem, "Young Charlotte lived on the mountain in a wild and lonely spot," but as it did not make much impression, he would trudge grimly to bed muttering about the foolishness of dancing all night and coming home in the cold hours of the morning. My mother, who danced plenty in her girlhood, would smile a little and keep on mending, seldom taking part in the discussion....

Who could ask for anything better than to be young and carefree, riding behind a sleek, fast-stepping chestnut horse, in a sleigh with plenty of warm robes, going to a dance with a considerate young escort with the moon making the snow glisten like bright crystals?

As we neared the farmhouse... lights glowed from the windows, casting shadows on the snow outside. Dogs barked with excitement and children of all ages ran about. The men congregated in the kitchen, while the ladies went into the other rooms and piled their wraps on the beds. There were always several youngsters mixed in with the coats, sleeping peacefully....

Finally the fiddler would arrive and be greeted warmly. Many times he would be given a chair high up by the iron sink, where his toes would be safe from the dancers. Next he usually had a good drink of hard cider to give him courage to begin. Then the folks would form for a Portland Fancy or Virginia Reel to start things off. The rafters of the old farmhouse would ring with the sounds of all kinds of jigs, reels and square dances. There would be laughter, and good rural friendship among the neighbors and many a courtship would have its beginning there.

Daisy Dopp

Daisy Dopp's Vermont,
1983

JONES'S PARING BEE

Susan Jane, do you remember
Down to Jones's paring bee,
When I took you and your brother
Along with Sally Green and me.

Yes, Josiah, I remember,
'Twas in wintertime you know:
We wandered along the highway
Then we went on through the snow.

When old Jones took up the fiddle,
Hallelujah, didn't he play?
Right and left and down the middle,
And we'd dance 'till break of day.

Too-ra-lee-ra, loo-ra-li-do
Too-ra-lee-ra, loo-ra-lee
Oh, what fun we had together
Down to Jones's paring bee.

As sung by

Margaret MacArthur

*An Almanac of New England
Farm Songs*, 1982

Clyde Hunter, Lyndonville.

Nancy Wasserman

MY POETIC CAREER IN VERMONT POLITICS

I found it at times necessary and helpful to break into therapeutic verse. The first occasion arose when a bill had been introduced to make the Morgan horse the official state animal. This was a nonpartisan measure; members of both parties rushed to sign it and identify themselves to the folks back home as friends of the Morgan. When the bill was in the General Committee, various other animals were proposed — the porcupine, the goat, the catamount, the cow. But it was decided in the end that the Morgan horse was the most acceptable.

Justin Morgan, a Randolph farmer and music teacher, received the colt that was progenitor of the remarkable Morgan line as payment for a debt in 1795. A descendant, left, gets its winter constitutional in Westford.

Dana C. Carlson

I agreed to speak and on the third reading of the bill read:

"A Minor Ode to the Morgan Horse"

I may not incline
to the porcupine,
And I may be averse
To what is much worse:
The bear,
That is rare,
The goat
That's remote,
The sheep, from which year after year
    you must remove the coat,
The catamount
That does not amount to that amount,
The cow,
That somehow
We, as a human minority, cannot allow:
And although, as one of the Democratic minority
    I should, alas,
Far prefer the jackass,
I must — until a state animal can choose
    its own state —
Not hesitate
To vote, of course,
For the Morgan horse.

William Jay Smith
1964

GOOD SECURITY

Solid of step and intention, a farmer escorts two draft horses to their stalls in East Corinth. Before mechanization, the work horse was general transportation, log skidder, tractor, and an all-around portable power source for generations of Vermont farmers. Today, they still work where machines can't be used.

William E. Hebden

Joe Hood, a rather unsuccessful farmer, came into the bank seeking to borrow five thousand dollars. He was interviewed in the private office of the vice-president and one of the loan officers.

"What security have you got, Joe?"

"Well, my farm and cattle," answered Joe.

"Tell me about your farm. How many acres are there? And what kind of land is it?"

"There are 150 acres. Twenty acres of hay land, and the rest is swamp, pasture, and woods."

"What is the pasture land like?"

"Well, it's pretty rocky and thin soil. I have to rent pasture in addition to keep my cows."

"What condition are the buildings in?"

"Oh, I'd say fair. Suit me. The house needs a new roof, and the chimney needs rebuilding. The porch sags some, and the underpinning is rotted on one side. Oh yes, it needs painting. But other than that it's quite comfortable."

"How about the barn?"

"Well, lightning struck one end of the roof. I ain't got around to fix it yet. One part of the floor on the south end has fallen in, but I figure I can do most of the work and fix that myself."

"How about your cows?"

"There's twenty of them. They haven't been tested for Bang's Disease yet. Five of them were barren last year. I gotta get rid of them, but I have been waiting for the price of beef to rise. Anymore I can tell you?" said Joe.

"No, I guess not," said the bank official.

"Well then," Joe asked, "what are you going to do? All I want to know is, do I get the loan? I don't want a lot of banker doubletalk. Just tell me yes or no."

"Okay," said the banker. "The answer is no."

"Thank you," said Hood, and he left the office.

A little later the banker came out of his office and noticed Hood standing at the cashier's window, apparently depositing money. Curious, he investigated and found that Hood had just deposited five thousand dollars in a savings account. When Hood left the window, the banker accosted him.

"Joe, what in the world is the idea? Here you are depositing five thousand dollars, and a few minutes ago you were trying to borrow five thousand."

"Well, you see, it's like this. I just received five thousand dollars that my uncle left me and I been wondering where to put it. So I thought I'd check up on this bank. When you told me right off you wouldn't make that loan on my security, I was pretty sure my money would be safe here."

Deane C. Davis

Nothing But the Truth,
1982

SPRING

JUG BROOK

After the travail of winter and the mess of mud season, spring comes to Strafford in a burst of flowing water and new leaves.

John Layton

Photograph Pages 140-141:

Barnet.

Richard W. Brown

Beyond the stone wall,
the deer should be emerging from their yard.
Lank, exhausted, they scrape at the ground
where roots and bulbs will send forth
new definitions. The creek swells in its ditch;
the field puts on a green glove.
Deep in the woods, the dead ripen,
and the lesser creatures turn to their commission.

Why grieve for the lost deer,
for the fish that clutter the brook,
the kingdoms of midge that cloud its surface,
the flocks of birds that come to feed.
The earth does not grieve.
It rushes toward the season of waste —

On the porch the weather shifts,
the cat dispatches
another expendable animal from the field.
Soon she will go inside to cull her litter,
addressing each with a diagnostic tongue.
Have I learned nothing? God,
into whose deep pocket our cries are swept,
it is you I look for
in the slate face of the water.

Ellen Bryant Voigt
The Forces of Plenty, 1983

Return to Vermont

At last the time came when we were bound back for the farm.... To us the 410 miles from New York City seemed a long grind, and even after we reached the south end of Vermont, we had more than 150 miles to go. Just at sunset we were rolling up the last stretch of road, seeing the quiet lake again, the maple trees and the white gable end of our house gleaming among the leaves.

We pulled up and tumbled onto the green grass beside the house, where we stretched out flat and pressed our noses into the green cool freshness of the grass roots. It was too good even to speak of. The sun sank down behind the western ridges across the lake, the bright blue of the sky dimmed, and it almost seemed we could feel the coolness of the dew quietly falling like a blessing....

Only time and the needs of a family can determine whether we'll be able to stay on our farm year-round or summers only, or whether we'll find ourselves looking for another small farm somewhere else, now that we've learned a little about it the hard way. Perhaps it doesn't matter. The sunset will still flame over the snowdrifts, and the beautiful blizzards will come roaring in from the northwest. The trees will lose their leaves and grow them again. The cow-slips will spring up in the swales and the violets in the woods. And in me and in my children, I hope, will be a consciousness that natural things are as powerful and all-pervading as they ever were in the time of the pagan Greeks and the wine-dark sea and the sylvan gods. The springtimes come, when the maple leaves unroll "as big as a mouse's ear;" the wild roses bloom; the blackberries ripen; and these things will go on, as the old New England land deeds phrase it, "as long as grass grows and water runs." It is good to know all this, for there is really nothing else.

Elliott Merrick

Green Mountain Farm,
1948

Tunbridge.

Hanson Carroll

ABOUT THE AUTHORS

Absher, Thomas D., 1938-. A professor at Vermont College in Montpelier and a resident of Plainfield, Absher earned his Ph.D. in English at the University of Pennsylvania. He came to Vermont in 1968 to teach at Goddard College in Plainfield. His books include *Forms of Praise* and *The Calling*.
"Gravity Feed," page 65; "August," page 75.

Aiken, George D., 1892-1984. A native of Putney, Vermont, in 1930 Aiken was elected to the Vermont House of Representatives, marking the start of a political career that led to the governorship of the state (1937-1941) and many terms as United States senator (1941-1975). His first vocation was that of nurseryman, however, and his book, *Pioneering with Wildflowers*, reflects his lifelong love of plants.
"Why Grow Wildflowers?" page 48.

Bancroft, Ernest Harrison, 1880-1945. Long a prominent figure in agriculture and public life in South Barre, Vermont, Bancroft was manager of the Granite City Cooperative Creamery, and president of New England Dairies. Except for his years at the Chicago Veterinary College, class of 1911, he spent his entire life in the Barre area.
"The Green Mountain Parkway: In Favor," page 105.

Bismarck, Otto von, 1815-1898. German statesman and first chancellor of the German empire. A Vermont visitor to Berlin, Dr. S. W. Thayer, was friendly with Bismarck and evidently answered many questions from the chancellor about government and politics in the state. Another doctor there at the time, Edward S. Breck, was the source of this anecdote.
"Bismarck on Vermont," page 47.

Budbill, David, 1940-. Budbill's poems, plays, and children's books reflect the people and places of northern Vermont, where he lives near the village of Wolcott. Titles include *The Chain Saw Dance, From Down to the Village, Why I Came to Judevine,* and *Christmas Tree Farm.* He has been an English teacher, forester, gardener, and carpenter's apprentice, and holds degrees from Muskingum College and Columbia University.
"Journey for the North," page 17; "Old Man Pike," p. 119.

Carruth, Hayden, 1921-. Carruth is a professor of English at Syracuse University. He lived in Johnson, Vermont, for twenty years, while a free-lance editor and reviewer. He is the author of more than twenty-five volumes of poetry, criticism, and fiction.
From "Vermont," page 6; "Marshall Washer," page 43.

Colburn, Francis, 1910-1984. Long-time chairman of the art department at the University of Vermont and artist-in-residence, Colburn was by avocation a humorist. His amusing parody of a commencement speech, called "A Graduation Address," is a Vermont classic. A native Vermonter, he was a resident of Burlington for most of his life.
"Mud Season," page 28; "A Parable," page 103.

Coolidge, Calvin, 1872-1933. Born and raised in Plymouth, Vermont, Coolidge embarked upon a political career that quickly took him away from his native state, although he returned often to his family's Vermont homestead. First a Massachusetts state senator, then governor of Massachusetts (1916-1918), and vice-president (1920-1923), Coolidge was sworn in as president of the United States in 1923 at his Plymouth farm on the death of President Harding. He came from a long line of Yankee farmers and storekeepers. Rural schools and St. Johnsbury Academy prepared him for Amherst College, which he entered in 1891. His son Calvin, Jr., died tragically at age sixteen.
"If I Had Not Been President," page 79; "Vermont is a State I Love," page 99.

Davis, Deane, 1900-. Davis, governor of Vermont from 1969-1972, was born in East Barre and resides in Montpelier. He received his law degree from Boston University Law School in 1922, practiced law in Vermont, and became a judge of the Superior Court. His books, *Justice in the Mountains* and *Nothin' But the Truth*, recount his experiences as a country lawyer.
"Good Security," page 138.

Dopp, Daisy, 1899-1981. Daisy Sherburne graduated from Barton Academy in 1917, and two years later married Jim Dopp of Sheffield. She worked on the family's large dairy farm and wrote columns about rural life for the *Newport Daily Express*. The Sherburne barn, built in Glover during the Civil War by Daisy's great-grandfather, now houses the Bread and Puppet Museum.
"Kitchen Junkets," page 134.

Wilmington.

Carol Simowitz

Duffus, Robert Luther, 1888-1972. Duffus was a distinguished journalist whose roots remained firmly fixed in the Waterbury, Vermont, of his childhood, even though he spent thirty-two years as an editorial writer and reporter for the *New York Times*. The son of a stonecutter, Duffus started his career at age thirteen, writing for local newspapers. His books, *The Waterbury Record* and *Williamstown Branch*, evoke small-town Vermont life at the turn of the century.
"The Stingiest Man," page 27.

Field, Eugene, 1850-1895. Field's parents were native Vermonters, (his father graduated from Middlebury College at age eleven) and as a boy Field spent summers at his grandmother's home in Newfane. Born in St. Louis, he grew up in Amherst, Massachusetts, and worked for various newspapers in the Midwest. He was a poet of sentiment and whimsy; his "Wynken, Blynken and Nod" and "Little Boy Blue," reputedly written after the death of his eldest son at age thirteen, are a permanent part of American children's literature.
"Steep Hills and Wild Strawberries," page 52.

Fisher, Dorothy Canfield, 1879-1958. A longtime resident of Arlington, Vermont, Dorothy Canfield received a Ph.D. in French from Columbia University and intended to become a language teacher until she met and married James Fisher. They traveled frequently to France, but spent most of their time on the Canfield farm of her forebears. "I have lived in Vermont ever since 1763," Mrs. Fisher wrote in her book, *Vermont Tradition*. A storyteller of consummate skill, Mrs. Fisher was the author of *The Bent Twig, Hillsboro People,* and *Understood Betsy,* a children's book published in 1916 and still in print, as well as many other novels and non-fiction works.
"Town Meeting," page 19. "Quiet," page 76.

Frost, Robert Lee, 1874-1963. Frost tried many trades — school teacher, cobbler, newspaper editor, farmer in Derry, New Hampshire — before he met success as a poet. After he moved to England in 1912, a London publisher, David Nutt, recognized Frost's unique voice and published his first books, *A Boy's Will* and *North of Boston.* Some years after Frost's return from England he moved to South Shaftsbury, Vermont. He lived to become America's most admired poet, his work widely known and loved. Summers he lectured at the Bread Loaf School at Middlebury College and lived in Ripton, Vermont.
"The Telephone," page 51; "The Last Word of a Bluebird," page 95; "My November Guest," page 107.

Guiterman, Arthur, 1871-1943. Guiterman wrote light verse and ballads based on American history and legends. His books include *The Light Guitar, Wildwood Fables,* and *I Sing the Pioneer.* Born in Vienna, he was educated at City College of New York, and frequently spent time in Vermont. He served on the editorial staff of the *Woman's Home Companion,* the *Literary Digest,* and other magazines.
"Windham Thaw," page 130.

Hard, Walter, 1882-1966. Born in Manchester, Vermont, one of the fifth generation of Hards to live in the Battenkill Valley, Hard ran the family drugstore in Manchester, and then the Johnny Appleseed Bookshop in the same town. He served five terms in the Vermont legislature (1937-1946) and was a columnist for the *Rutland Herald* for many years.
"The Village," page 87.

Hawthorne, Nathaniel, 1804-1864. The author of *The Scarlet Letter* and *The House of the Seven Gables* made occasional trips from his home in Massachusetts to northern New England. In 1835 he came to Burlington on a walking tour, and some months later published his impressions of the city in *New England Magazine.*
"A Visit to Burlington," page 70.

Hayford, James, 1913-. Hayford's poems have appeared in *Harper's, Saturday Evening Post, The New Yorker,* and other magazines. He is a native Vermonter and a resident of Orleans, Vermont, who has taught school at every level from first grade through college, and been a musician, farmer, carpenter, and textbook editor. He holds degrees from Amherst College and Columbia University. In 1987 his first children's book, *Gridley Firing,* a Vermont story, was published.
"Processional with Wheelbarrow," page 39; "Harvesting the Squash," page 82; "Time to Plant Trees," page 100; "Love of Snow," page 132.

Hemenway, Abby Maria, 1828-1890. Born in Ludlow, Vermont, by 1858 this remarkable woman had published a highly acclaimed anthology, *Poets and Poetry of Vermont.* Her next proposal — to compile a history of her state — met with disapproval, however; such a plan was considered unwomanly. Despite hostility, lack of funds, and creditors who seized the books, Hemenway completed nearly five volumes of her history before she died. It took almost thirty years and four million words. Today *The Vermont Historical Gazetteer* is judged a historic treasure, coveted by scholars and collectors of Vermontiana.
"A City's Spirit," page 73.

Hoagland, Edward, 1932-. Harvard-educated Hoagland is an essayist, short story writer, and novelist. He is a part-time resident of Barton, Vermont, writes the nature editorials for the *New York Times,* of which *"Songs and Snakeskins"* was one, and has taught at Bennington College. His books include *Seven Rivers West, Red Wolves and Black Bears, Walking the Dead Diamond River,* and *The Tugman's Passage.*
"Songs and Snakeskins," page 30.

Huntington, Lee Pennock, 1918-. Lee Huntington is a children's book writer, essayist, and book reviewer. Her ancestors founded Strafford, Vermont. She served with her husband on a Quaker relief team in North Africa and as a member of the Religious Society of Friends' (Quaker) delegation to the United Nations. She lives on the Rochester farm that she writes about so eloquently in *Hill Song.*
"A Certain Comfort," page 109.

Johnson, Charles W., 1943-. Johnson, Vermont's state naturalist, writes about natural history from his East Montpelier home. His books include *The Nature of Vermont* and *Bogs of the Northeast.* His work with the Vermont Department of Forests, Parks and Recreation has involved management of natural areas, protection of endangered species, and acquisition of public lands such as Mt. Hunger, Woods Island in Lake Champlain, and Camp Plymouth State Park.
"A Place for Strange Gods," page 35.

Kappel-Smith, Diana, 1951-. A writer with a passionate interest in the natural world, Ms. Kappel-Smith ran a 275-acre farm in Wolcott, Vermont, for several years. She attended Sarah Lawrence College and graduated from the University of Vermont with a degree in botany.
"Falling Off," page 89.

Kent, Louise Andrews, 1886-1969. Kents' Corner, a rural crossroads in Calais, Vermont, was the summer home of the Kent family for many years. There Mrs. Kent wrote children's books (*He Went with Champlain, He Went with Magellan,* etc.) as well as her popular "Mrs. Appleyard" cooking columns for the *Ladies Home Journal* and *Vermont Life.* Her cookbooks — among them, *Mrs. Appleyard's Family Kitchen* and *Mrs. Appleyard's Kitchen* — were a felicitous mixture of recipes and deft commentary on the domestic affairs of the Kent family.
"Mrs. Appleyard's Apple-Tree Cheese," page 54.

Kinnell, Galway, 1927-. A summer resident of Sheffield, Vermont, Kinnell was born in Rhode Island and educated at Princeton University. He taught English at many colleges, including New York University and the University of Grenoble. In 1983 he received both the American Book Award and the Pulitzer Prize for poetry, and he has published over twenty books of poetry, a novel, essays and translations.
"Ruins Under the Stars," page 81; "A Winter Sky," page 111.

Lawrence, Andrea Mead, 1932-. "My parents dreamed a mountain and bought it," wrote Rutland-born Andrea Mead Lawrence about Pico Peak. "They made it into a resort where I learned to ski." In 1952 in Oslo, Mead became the first American to win two Olympic gold medals in skiing. She writes of her love for Pico, skiing, climbing, and family in her autobiographical *A Practice of Mountains.*
"Mountain Philosophy," page 123.

Leslie, Hyde, 1852-1948. We know little about this Vermonter who wrote so sparingly of his experiences in 1887, when he worked as a hired man for James S. Brown in Plymouth, Vermont. He did odd jobs for town residents, farmed, and died at the Odd Fellows Home in Ludlow at age ninety-six.
"A Winter Diary," page 115.

Wells.

Paul O. Boisvert

149

Lewis, Sinclair, 1885-1951. Lewis was awarded the Nobel prize for literature in 1930, the first American author so honored. He traveled often, rarely spending more than eight months in any spot. But he owned a farm in Barnard, Vermont, and Vermont was the first place he had seen where he really wanted to have his home — "a place," he said, "to spend the rest of my life."
"Vermont's Virtues," page 41.

MacArthur, Margaret, 1928-. A collector and performer of New England songs and rhymes, Margaret MacArthur has lived for thirty years in the same Marlboro, Vermont, farmhouse. Time spent restoring the house, built in the early 1800s, gave her insight into the life of her predecessors, as did tilling the scant soil to raise food for her family of seven. These experiences influenced her to look for songs that expressed New England farm life, at a time, she says, when "people lived not half so fast."
"Maple Sweet," page 25; "Dried Apple Pies," page 121; "Jones's Paring Bee," page 135.

Marsh, George Perkins, 1801-1882. A lawyer, farmer, businessman, and scholar, Marsh was raised in Woodstock, Vermont, and went on to an international career that combined writing, scholarship, and politics. He produced such diverse works as *A Compendious Grammar of the Old-Northern or Icelandic Language* and *Man and Nature,* an 1864 plea for the peaceful coexistence of man with his environment, now considered the fountainhead of the conservation movement. While a member of the U.S. House of Representatives, he helped pass the legislation that created the Smithsonian Institution. He also served as minister to Turkey (1849-54) and Italy (1860-82), where he spent the last twenty-one years of his life.
"The Given Earth," page 33.

McCarriston, Linda, 1943-. Writer, mother, teacher of English, Linda McCarriston moved to Plainfield, Vermont, in 1979 to marry poet Tom Absher. *Talking Soft Dutch* is her first published book of poetry. She was born in Lynn, Massachusetts, and received a Master of Fine Arts in writing from Goddard College.
"Spring," page 36.

Merrick, Elliott, 1901-. Merrick homesteaded near Craftsbury, Vermont, with his young family in the 1930s. He taught at Craftsbury Academy, the University of Vermont, and later at Black Mountain College in North Carolina. He is the author of *Green Mountain Farm, From This Hill Look Down,* and *Northern Nurse,* an account of his wife's experiences with the Grenfell Mission in Labrador. He and his wife now live in Ashville, North Carolina.
"On Lake Champlain," page 67; "Drifts of Leaves," page 102; "Snowy Afternoon," page 129; "Return to Vermont," page 145.

Mosher, Howard Frank, 1942-. Mosher's novels and short stories — *Where the Rivers Flow North, Marie Blythe,* and *Disappearances* — focus on the harshness of life in northern Vermont and the resourcefulness of the people who live there. He is a resident of Irasburg, and in 1981 he received the Literature Award of the American Academy and Institute of Arts and Letters.
"The View from the Hill," page 90.

Nearing, Scott, 1883-1983, and Nearing, Helen, 1903-. The Nearings wrote about their Jamaica, Vermont, experiences in *Living the Good Life* (1950) and *The Maple Sugar Book* (1970), both full of congenial advice on how to live in harmony with the land. In 1952, "after the ski industry and summer tourists threatened to engulf... their quiet valley," they moved to Maine. Until Scott Nearing's death at age 100, they divided their time between farming and dispensing their special philosophy to thousands of visitors, and traveling and lecturing throughout the world.
"Making Do," page 59.

Needham, Walter, 1896-. An auto mechanic, factory worker, and jack-of-all-trades, Walter Needham is a Vermonter whose ancestors settled the state in 1794. He lives in Guilford and was the grandson of Leroy L. Bond, the "Gramp" in *A Book of Country Things,* who taught him the practical skills of frontier America described in this oral history.
"Plowing, Harrowing and Planting," page 61.

Peach, Arthur Wallace, 1886-1956. Peach, a native Vermonter and Middlebury College graduate, was a Norwich University faculty member for thirty-seven years and lived most of his life in Northfield, Vermont. He was on the editorial board of *Vermont Life,* and his column, "At the Sign of the Quill," appeared regularly in the magazine. He was a member of the Historic Sites Commission, president of the Better Library Movement, which created Vermont's innovative regional library system, and director of the Vermont Historical Society. "Vermont is the state in the Union nearest paradise," he was fond of saying.
"The Green Mountain Parkway: Against," page 105.

Perkins, Nathan, 1749-18??. Reverend Perkins attended Princeton University and was graduated with the class of 1770. He was minister of the Third Church of West Hartford, Connecticut, for sixty-five years. It was from Connecticut that he made his trip to Vermont.
"A Visitor's Opinion," page 93.

Perrin, Noel, 1927-. Dartmouth College English professor since 1959, writer, part-time farmer, and longtime resident of Thetford Center, Vermont, Perrin's work has been published in the *New York Times, Vermont Life, Country Journal,* and the *Washington Post.* He was born in New York City.
"The First Good Run," page 21; "A Cool Morning in Vermont," page 125.

Smith, William Jay, 1918-. Smith is a poet, children's book author, critic, and editor. He has also taught French and English literature. He was a Democratic member of Vermont House of Representatives, 1960-62, while living in North Pownal. "My Poetic Career in Vermont Politics," page 137.

Starbird, Kaye, 1916-. Kaye Starbird was born in Fort Sill, Oklahoma, and lives in Peterborough, New Hampshire. She is a graduate of the University of Vermont and has written poetry, essays, short stories, and children's books.
"The Covered Bridge House," page 94.

Taggard, Genevieve, 1894-1948. Genevieve Taggard was a Washington State native who grew up in Hawaii and taught at Mt. Holyoke, Bennington, and Sarah Lawrence colleges. She lived in East Jamaica, Vermont, and her books of poetry include *A Part of Vermont* and *Slow Music.* Some of her poems were set to music by composers William Schuman and Aaron Copland.
"The Nursery Rhyme and the Summer Visitor," page 57.

Voigt, Ellen Bryant, 1943-. Ellen Voigt attended Converse College in South Carolina and the Writers' Workshop at the University of Iowa. A resident of Cabot, Vermont, she is the author of *Claiming Kin,* which *The Nation* called a "stunning first collection," *The Forces of Plenty,* and *The Lotus Flowers.* She is a visiting faculty member in the M.F.A. Program for Writers at Warren Wilson College in North Carolina.
"Jug Brook," page 143.

Wetherell, W.D., 1948-. Wetherell's fiction and non-fiction have appeared in the *New York Times, The Atlantic, Country Journal,* and *Vermont Life.* He has won two O. Henry Awards for his short stories and is the author of a novel, *Souvenirs.* In 1985 he received the Drue Heinz Literature Prize for a collection of short stories, *The Man Who Loved Levittown.* He is a resident of Lyme, New Hampshire.
"A Golden Moment," page 97.

Acknowledgments

"August," p. 75, and "Gravity Feed," p. 65, are reprinted by permission from *Forms of Praise* by Tom Absher. Copyright © 1981 by the Ohio State University Press, Columbus. All rights reserved.

"Why Grow Wildflowers?" p. 48, is reprinted from *Pioneering with Wildflowers* by George D. Aiken, The Countryman Press, Woodstock, VT, 1968, p. 1, 2. Reprinted by permission of the publisher.

"Journey for the North," p. 17, is reprinted from *Down to the Village* by David Budbill, New York, 1981. Reprinted by permission of the author.

"Old Man Pike," p. 119, is reprinted from *The Chain Saw Dance* by David Budbill, The Countryman Press, Woodstock, VT, 1977. Reprinted by permission of the author.

The quotation from the poem "Vermont," p. 6, and "From Marshall Washer," p. 43, are reprinted from *Brothers, I Loved You All* by Hayden Carruth, Sheep Meadow Press, New York, 1978, p. 47 and pp. 63-64. Reprinted by permission of the author.

"Mud Season," p. 28, and "A Parable," p. 103, are reprinted from *Letters Home and Further Indiscretions* by Francis Colburn. Copyright 1978 by the New England Press, Shelburne, VT, p 56-58. Reprinted by permission of the publisher.

"If I Had Not Been President," p. 79, is reprinted from *The Autobiography of Calvin Coolidge*, Academy Books, Rutland, VT, 1972, pp. 189-190. Reprinted by permission of the Calvin Coolidge Memorial Foundation, Plymouth, VT.

"Good Security," p. 138, is reprinted from *Nothin' But the Truth* by Deane C. Davis. Copyright 1982 by the New England Press, Shelburne, VT, pp. 97-98. Reprinted with the permission of the publisher.

"Kitchen Junkets," p. 134, is reprinted from *Daisy Dopp's Vermont* by Daisy Dopp, Orleans County Historical Society, Brownington, VT, 1983, p. 84. Reprinted by permission of the publisher.

"The Stingiest Man," p. 27, is reprinted from *Williamstown Branch* by Robert Duffus, 1958, W. W. Norton and Company, New York, pp. 40-41.

"Town Meeting," p. 19, is reprinted from *Vermont Tradition* by Dorothy Canfield Fisher, copyright 1953 by Dorothy Canfield Fisher, published by Little Brown and Company, Boston. Reprinted by permission of the publisher.

"Quiet," p. 76, by Dorothy Canfield Fisher is reprinted from *The Lady from Vermont* by Elizabeth Yates, Stephen Greene Press, Brattleboro, VT, 1971, p. 180. Reprinted by permission of the publisher.

"Windham Thaw," p. 130, by Arthur Guiterman, "Maple Sweet," p. 25, and "Jones's Paring Bee," p. 135, are reprinted by permission of the Flanders Collection, Middlebury College, Middlebury, VT.

"My November Guest," p. 107, copyright 1934, © 1969 by Holt, Rinehart and Winston, Inc. Copyright © 1962 by Robert Frost; "The Telephone," p. 51, and "The Last Word of a Bluebird," p. 95, are reprinted from *The Poetry of Robert Frost* edited by Edward Connery Lathem. Copyright 1916, © 1969 by Holt, Rinehart and Winston. Copyright 1944 by Robert Frost. Reprinted by permission of Henry Holt and Company, Inc., New York.

"The Village," p. 87, is reprinted from *A Matter of Fifty Houses* by Walter Hard, 1952, Vermont Books, Middlebury, VT. Reprinted by permission of the publisher.

"Processional with Wheelbarrow," p. 39, is reprinted from *The Furniture of Earth* by James Hayford, Oriole Books, Orleans, VT, 1976. Reprinted by permission of the author.

"Harvesting the Squash," p. 82; "Time to Plant Trees," p. 100; and "Love of Snow," p. 132, are reprinted from *At Large on the Land* by James Hayford, Oriole Books, Orleans, VT, pp. 44, 72. Reprinted by permission of the author.

"Songs and Snakeskins," p. 30, is reprinted from *The Tugman's Passage* by Edward Hoagland. Copyright © 1976, 1977, 1978, 1979, 1980, 1982 by Edward Hoagland, p. 196. Reprinted by permission of Random House, Inc., New York.

"A Certain Comfort," p. 109, is reprinted from *Hill Song, A Country Journal* by Lee Pennock Huntington, p. 115, The Countryman Press, Woodstock, VT, 1985. Copyright © 1985 by Lee Pennock Huntington. Reprinted with permission.

153

BOOKS FOR FURTHER READING

Bassett, T. D. Seymour, *Outsiders Inside Vermont*. Canaan, NH: Phoenix Publishing, 1967.
Three centuries of visitors' viewpoints on the Green Mountain State — from Samuel de Champlain and Ethan Allen to Henry David Thoreau and John Updike.

Biddle, Arthur W., and Paul A. Eschholz, eds., *The Literature of Vermont*. Hanover, NH: University Press of New England, 1973.
An excellent survey of Vermont prose and poetry.

Cooley, Oscar, *When Grandpa Was a Boy*. Montpelier, VT: Vermont Historical Society, 1985.
Growing up on a farm in Randolph in the early years of the twentieth century — what it was like to fix fence, hoe corn, sugar, hay and thresh, milk the cows, harness the horse, and attend the village school.

Duffus, Robert, *Williamstown Branch*. New York: W. W. Norton, 1958.
———, *The Waterbury Record*. New York: W. W. Norton, 1959.
A *New York Times* reporter recalls his boyhood in Vermont in the early 1900s.

Fisher, Dorothy Canfield, *Vermont Tradition*. Boston: Little Brown, 1953.
An intensely personal statement about Vermont and what it means to the author.

Foley, Allen R., *What the Old-Timer Said, And Then Some! To the Feller From Down Country and Even to His Neighbor (When He Had It Coming)*. Illustrated by John Devaney. New York: Viking Penquin, 1983.
The snappers, whoppers, and comic tales associated with that state of mind called Vermont.

Goodman, Lee Dana, *Vermont Saints & Sinners*. Shelburne, VT: New England Press, 1985.
Lively essays limn an impressive assortment of geniuses, nincompoops, curmudgeons, scurvy knaves, and characters.

Hill, Ralph Nading, Murray Hoyt, and Walter R. Hard, Jr., *Vermont: A Special World*. Montpelier, VT: Vermont Life Magazine, 1968.
A flawless blend of history, humor, social commentary, and beautiful color photographs make this book a Vermont classic.

Hoagland, Edward, *The Tugman's Passage*. New York: Random House, 1981.
This fine collection of essays includes some eloquent writing on Vermont.

Huntington, Lee Pennock, *Hill Song*. Woodstock, VT: Countryman Press, 1985.
A calendar of comments on the Vermont year as the author views it with an exacting, sensitive eye from her farm in Rochester.

Jennison, Keith, *Vermonters and the State They're In*. Shelburne, VT: New England Press, 1985.
Pictures and telling phrases reveal a way of life, the flavor of an earlier Vermont.

———, *"Yup... Nope" & Other Vermont Dialogues*. Photographs by Neil Rappaport. Woodstock, VT: Countryman Press, 1976.
Wry commentary on the character of Vermonters.

Kent, Louise Andrews, *Mrs. Appleyard's Family Kitchen*. Montpelier, VT: Vermont Life Magazine, 1977.
A cookbook with over 700 recipes from several generations of the Kent family, interspersed with Mrs. Appleyard's humor, delight in the gatherings of friends, and the traditional life of Vermont's countryside.

Lawrence, Gale, *Vermont Life's Guide to Fall Foliage*. Montpelier, VT: Vermont Life Magazine, 1984.
A practical, pocket-sized guide to the colorful trees of New England as they appear in autumn.

Merrick, Elliott, *Green Mountain Farm*. Barton, VT: Sherry Urie Books, 1978, reprint.
The author's experiences homesteading in Vermont in the 1930s. Part of this book appeared originally in the *New Yorker*.

Mosher, Howard Frank, *Where the Rivers Flow North*. New York: Viking Penguin, 1985.
Six striking tales of everyday life in rural New England.

Perrin, Noel, *First Person Rural*. Boston: David R. Godine, 1978.
———, *Second Person Rural*. Boston: David R. Godine, 1980.
———, *Third Person Rural*. Boston: David R. Godine, 1983.
A fine defense of country living, not as a retreat from the world but as a place to use one's talents to battle it out.

Schwenke, Karl, *In a Pig's Eye*. Chelsea, VT: Chelsea Green Publishing, 1985.
First-rate pig tales and farming stories, some amusing, others moving, by a superb writer.

Slayton, Tom, *Finding Vermont.*
Montpelier, VT: *Vermont Life*
Magazine, 1986.
An informal guide to Vermont's places
and people by the editor of *Vermont
Life.*

Vachon, Brian, ed., *Vermont for
Every Season.* Montpelier, VT: *Vermont
Life* Magazine, 1980.
Color photos and text illumine
Vermont's distinctive seasons.

Wetherell, W. D., *Vermont River.*
New York: Nick Lyons Books, 1984.
A year in the life of a writer and
fisherman and a celebration of the
natural world of a river valley.

POETRY

East Corinth.

William Hebden

These poetry collections all reflect in
varying ways the Vermont experiences
of their authors.

Absher, Tom, *The Calling.* Cambridge,
MA: Alice Jones Press, 1987.

———, *Forms of Praise.* Columbus,
OH: Ohio State University Press, 1981.

Budbill, David, *Down to the Village.*
New York: The Ark 15, 1981.

———, *The Chain Saw Dance.*
Johnson, VT: Crow's Mark Press, 1976.

Carruth, Hayden, *If You Call This
Cry a Song.* Woodstock, VT:
Countryman Press, 1983.

———, *Brothers, I loved You All.*
New York: Sheep Meadow Press, 1978.

Frost, Robert, *The Poetry of Robert
Frost.* Edward C. Lathem, New York:
Holt, Rinehart & Winston, 1968.

Hard, Walter, *Walter Hard's Vermont
People.* Middlebury, VT: Vermont
Books, 1981.

———, *A Matter of Fifty Houses.*
Middlebury, VT: Vermont Books, 1952,
reprint.

Hayford, James, *The Furniture of
Earth.* Orleans, VT: Oriole Books, 1976.

———, *At Large On the Land.* Orleans,
VT: Oriole Books, 1983.

Kinnell, Galway, *Selected Poems.*
Boston: Houghton Mifflin, 1982.

McCarriston, Linda, *Talking Soft
Dutch.* Lubbock, TX: Texas Tech
Press, 1984.

Voigt, Ellen Bryant, *The Lotus Flowers.*
New York: W.W. Norton, 1987.

———, *The Forces of Plenty.* New York:
W. W. Norton, 1983.

———, *Claiming Kin.* Middletown,
CT: Wesleyan University Press, 1976.

Susan Bartlett Weber

Susan Bartlett Weber lives with her family in a farmhouse on two hundred acres in Calais, Vermont. She attended Wellesley College and received a B.A. degree from the University of Michigan. A former editor for several New York publishers, she now serves as managing editor for the Vermont Historical Society in Montpelier. She is the author of two books on history for children and teaches writing workshops at the University of Vermont. The *Vermont Experience* is her first anthology.

Tom Slayton

Prior to becoming editor of *Vermont Life* Magazine, Tom Slayton was a reporter, bureau chief, and editor for the *Rutland Herald* and the Barre-Montpelier *Times-Argus*. He worked for Vermont newspapers for twenty years and won awards from the Vermont Press Association and the New England Press Association. In 1985, he was appointed editor of *Vermont Life*. He is a native of Vermont and lives in Montpelier with his wife, Elizabeth, and son, Ethan.

Book design by
The Laughing Bear Associates,
Montpelier, Vermont